THE PATH TO THE UNKNOWN

AHMED KHALAF

INK START MEDIA
5710 W Gate City Blvd Ste K #284
Greensboro, NC 27407

The Path to The Unknown

The events of my life are just totally insane; I myself the owner of this life can't even still believe what I have been through and still going through.

My story deals with Love, Friendships, Family, Education, Embassies, Governments and Corrupted Officials, Kidnapping, Lost Dreams, Marriages and Divorces, Multi Cultures and Languages, Religions, Residency and Citizenships, Effects of War, and Political Situations on my personal life and so much more.

At this very point in my life, I don't know yet what the ending will be. Will I succeed, will things turn out better, and will I be able to solve the mystery of these continuous events? I have no idea, but I am hopeful that while you read through my book the events of my life start changing towards becoming better.

I will start from the very beginning so that things will make sense and become clear. My name is Ahmed Khalaf, born in Germany on May 31, 1970. I was raised there and simply could say that I spent the 10 most amazing years of my life; I had a great childhood with a lot of wonderful memories. I am even still in touch with my childhood friends, something that we can call "True Friendship."

Being raised in Europe and in a place that is amazingly green; a country that teaches the importance of time and makes it its ultimate system that people naturally follow makes a child like me who grew up in a place like that, admire every single moment that could be remembered. These days have been always replayed in my head after the time my parents decided that they will take us (me and my two sisters) to Jordan.

As children, we didn't even know what Jordan is and where it was. All I knew was that my parents will take us somewhere and that somewhere was just far from my friends, school, and community. I still can remember very clearly when all of my friends came to say goodbye, tears never stopped falling, facing pain as early as a 10 year old boy. But what I didn't know was that what was coming was far worse and far more painful, but how could I? I was just a little kid.

The day has come when I, my mom, and my two younger sisters landed in Jordan, my dad stayed behind in Germany, and my life just went downwards from that point on, I was in a total culture shock, from a green country to a desert, from German and English speaking to Arabic, a language that I didn't know, a language that sounded so hard. To me, it felt like being taken out from Paradise to Hell for reasons I didn't know, didn't understand, and even refused to have it justified.

In order to fit into this new life and community I had to work so hard on learning Arabic, and despite of that I was never totally accepted, I can still hear the voices that were saying: "here comes Ahmed the German, here goes Ahmed the German". And on top of that, I was even bullied from time to time; I just wasn't brought up that way.

Two years later I flew back to Germany to visit my dad and my friends, my first international flight at the age of 12 totally alone, just being escorted by Lufthansa Airlines personnel. It felt so great, just imagine someone who was deprived of breathing and then given a moment to catch a breath again.

The tears of joy being back home were just beyond description, I had an amazing three months with my friends and my dad, but as usual, good times always end so quickly and before you know it, time is up, and misery has to start again.

And YES, it wasn't enough for destiny to throw me back to the place I didn't want to be at, it had to mess me up more and more.

Three years later and at the age of (15) I met a guy who was my classmate and my competitor in class, we became very close friends. At the end of the school year, he requested me to do him a small favor by dropping by his house to give his books to his mom; he had to stay longer in school for some errands. So I agreed because I wanted to actually meet my best friend's family in Jordan. I took the request of my friend with joy and made my way to his house, I rang the bell and when the door opened, I was in a complete state of silence, I can still feel the blood running up my cheeks making them red, my heart was beating so fast that I didn't understand what was going on with me. It was the unexpected; the door was opened by an Angel and not the mother of my friend, a very pretty girl with the most amazing smile I've ever seen. I was so nervous that my tongue wouldn't move to talk. I still can remember the exact words she told me with her smiling face "Can I help you?" I had to get out of my freezing mode and replied, "I am here to drop off these books; I assume he would be your brother" a voice from inside shouted "who's this?" And she replied, "it's my brother's friend". The mother came out and was so very polite and invited me in. But I was so shy that I apologized and excused myself by promising that I would come by during the school holiday to have lunch someday. The mother smiled and stated that I would be always welcome.

Honestly, at that moment I thought that things would be just alright, and that life will smile on my face once again, a bit weird for a 15-year-old to think that way, but the pain I had from leaving Germany never disappeared.

A few days passed and my best friend called up inviting me for lunch, I was really happy. That was the time I was introduced to the entire family, and I got to see that Angel once again. I spent the entire day with them, and it felt like I am having a new life. From that day on I kept visiting my new family, my second family and my feelings got stronger and stronger for that Angel.

A whole year passed, and my dad decided to finally follow us to Jordan and left Germany permanently, why? I have no clue, but he came. I was 16 years old back then. After a few days after my dad's arrival the entire family of my friend came to our house for the first time, so it became a family relationship. That was a night that I will never forget in my life because it was the night that I had the chance to be alone with the Angel on the balcony and tell her frankly with no hesitation that I loved her from the bottom of my heart. She on the other hand just smiled and blushed but didn't say anything at all.

The relationship secretly went on and I kind of felt bad about it, due to cultural differences I felt as if I was cheating on my friend by not telling him that I fell in love with his sister, I felt bad because this family opened their door for me but I am loving their daughter secretly, I knew that I am not in Germany and that the culture and the way of living are just so different in Jordan, so I wanted to make it right. So, one day I waited until my friend went to school ahead of me and I went to their house, his mother opened the door for me, and she was surprised that I was late for school and told me that her son left already. So I smiled and told her that I knew that; and my reason for being late was to talk to her. She made coffee and told me these exact words "what is it my son?" so I told her that I was part of the family already and that my upbringing was just different from the people of this country, she looked at me puzzled and told me to just say what was bothering me, she was such an understanding woman. So, with extreme difficulty, I let it out and told her that I was in love with her daughter and that I couldn't hide this from her in particular. She smiled and told me "Son, just focus on your studies for now, and whenever the right time comes these things could be discussed, you are still too young" when she saw me kind of disappointed she added "but I promise you, if you do well and it's your destiny to be with her, I will be the first one to stand with you and help you".

I took these encouraging words and went to school; I had so much will to prove her and everybody else that I am smart and that I am really good in school. And with that I started studying like crazy, it's so strange what love can do to a person!

I finished my 11th grade with many ups and downs; my love for the Angel grew and grew despite of many obstacles. My meetings with my love were limited because of the culture that doesn't really allow it. Nevertheless, I managed to keep going and started my last and most crucial school year, the year that I should pass with flying marks to qualify for the University, the year that will make me shine in front of my Angel's mom. I was so ready for the year, I was so excited for it, but what I didn't know was that another heavy trial was waiting for me, that another hit from heavens will fall on my head.

Supposedly I should have adapted to life in Jordan, supposedly I should be OK with having love in my life and having my family together, and supposedly I should be ready to plan my future since I already knew what I wanted, but it seems that nothing in life works as we want, it doesn't really matter how well we plan things, if it's not meant to be then it will never happen, but how can a teenager even know all of that?

A half-sister of my mother was a jealous devil, she was jealous of our family and how we were different, she was comparing her kids with us, we were so much into studying and her kids were just running away from school, even the lifestyle and the understanding we had as a family was an issue to her. I never loved this creature despite that I never knew before that she was a really bad person, and that she had a long long-planned plan.

The timing indeed was extremely terrible; this was a year that I had to fully concentrate on, but that just wasn't possible, this half-sister of my mom whom I don't even acknowledge as an aunt made her move and came in between my dad and mom, somehow she managed to make my dad believe that my mother was seeing someone else, that she was in a relationship, what an Irony, we were living in a society where that was even impossible, so how did my dad even fall for that? How did he let this nonsense go through his head? I even started doubting that he lived in Germany for 25 years. The problem escalated and my mother was so offended and hurt, she even pointed out that if ever she wanted such a thing, she would've done so when my dad was still in Germany for 6 full years before he joined us.

All these days, weeks, and months of continuous problems affected me big time and my study habits, it affected my willingness, and my mood, and the results couldn't be any less obvious, I flanked the first semester. This further led to a non-pleasant environment with my Angel, and it felt as if the entire universe was falling on my head. I didn't know what to do. My family on one side, my beloved one on the other, and my crushed dream of having great scores in the most crucial year of my school life on top of all. I didn't know what to do. I was crushed at this very stage of my life, I felt so bad that I was hoping to die and have it all ended. But instead, my agony was prolonged, and I had to make a decision, either surrender as early as then, or make these problems make me stronger in one way or the other, so I decided to ignore both of my family problems and even my Angel, at least for the period of the second semester. And so it was,

I studied really hard and just kept my distance from everyone and everything until the second semester ended and my hard work paid off, I was able to make up for my failing scores in the first semester and passed the year, however, and unfortunately, the grade wasn't high at all, which meant I couldn't study at a Government University in Jordan; and so I had to find a way to study abroad in a country that was not too expensive.

It was my mission to search and ask; I just refused to stay in Jordan not being able to study and on top of that in an environment that was not conducive to living. After almost 3 months I had the options of East Germany, Russia, and Hungary, that was my time to convince my dad that he had to support me, it was because of him and my mom in the first place that I was facing all of this. After a long give and take my dad agreed and the choice fell on Hungary. And with that, I flew to Budapest in September 1988; this was the second time to travel on my own during my 18 years of life. From Budapest, I took the train to a city named Miskolc and my new education journey started.

I was a student at NME (University of Miskolc), it was a hard start, just as any new start and the language barrier was really an obstacle, very limited people spoke English, and none spoke any German. So the solution was to learn Hungarian soon as possible, therefore; I decided to shift from studying in English to Hungarian. I think due to what I have faced so far, I always pushed myself to a challenge. The days passed and I was happy being a University Student, but I think prolonged happiness for some reason was just forbidden for me, I received a phone call from my dad informing me that he and mom got divorced, but the news didn't shock me really, it was quite anticipated. My dad was poisoned with wrong thoughts, and my mom was hurt, big-time offended and extremely stubborn to even think of letting it slide. So the only anticipated outcome was their divorce.

Nevertheless, I continued my life and tried not to bother myself much because I just wanted to achieve my goal and be successful. My life in Eastern Europe was great and I loved it there, but I didn't dare to find a girlfriend because my heart and thoughts were totally with my Angel in Jordan, I wanted to surprise her, her family, and my family with my achievements, I wanted to prove that what happened during my last school year was not my fault.

I made really well in my studies and learned Hungarian within 6 months; I was even exempted from taking the final Language Exam because I had a full mark in all of my tests and exams.

One day and before my final test in Physics, something in my head told me to go and check the box where students receive their mails, it was a weird feeling really, especially since the anxiety that I had was so high prior to the exam, but I went with my guts and checked for mails and my gut was never so right as this time. But I was too surprised, and I didn't believe it, I even had to wash my face and rub my eyes, yet it still was the same, the sender was the love of my life, my Angel, her first International letter ever. From the extreme joy that I had, I totally forgot about my Final Physics Exam, and I started reading the letter and repeating it over and over again until it was time to enter class for the exam. I honestly can't remember how and what I wrote during this exam, my mind was just floating in a different world.

A few days later the professor brought in the results and was really serious, he stated that never in the history of his classes had anyone managed to get a full mark and that a passing grade is already an achievement. All the students were listening carefully, and everybody wanted to know if they made it or not. And then, he said, "Who's Ahmed Khalaf?"

I was like "Oh Oh" what mess have I done? So I raised my hand and stood up and was fearful of the words that he might throw at me, but it was a moment of no escape. The professor then said "you are no longer school kids, but even though I request from all of you to clap your hands for Ahmed, he's the only student so far who managed to get a full mark in my class."

It doesn't matter how much I describe this moment; I won't be able to describe it the way it was, and I won't be able to describe the happiness and mixed feelings and emotions that I had. It was one of the best moments in my life. The power of Love is just simply amazing.

But for how long?

I didn't know that I had to answer such a question ever, the more I didn't know that I had to answer it as soon as I returned to Jordan after I finished my first University Year in 1989. When I arrived in Jordan; I was confident and had my head up and proud, ready to have a good time with my family despite being broken. Sadly, I was wrong, totally wrong. I was welcomed with disaster news; my family tried to hide it from me, but I was just persistent and wanted to know how my Angel was doing. Maybe I shouldn't have asked. But how could I? I missed her like crazy and was looking forward meeting her more than anyone else. But I was simply destined to be hit by life once more and this time right into the core of my heart, my Angel was forced to get married due to family issues where she was threatened by a stupid uneducated uncle of hers, that if she doesn't get married, her face will be burned by Acid. So, in order for her to save her own family, herself and an outbreak, she sacrificed herself. And I was the victim who totally got crushed. Why does life have to be like that?

I didn't know how my feet took me to their house, a walk of 20 minutes felt like a century, and when I arrived, I was welcomed very warmly but I was just crying and crying and I asked, "is it true?" and I repeated the same question over and over again until I woke up in a hospital wherein, I fainted and didn't know what happened anymore. My family and my second family were around me when I woke up, but as soon as my eyes opened and saw them all around me, I just couldn't stop from crying, and all of them were crying with me afterwards. The mother of my Angel tried to comfort me and said, "you'll find who's better than my daughter" and that just made me vomit and the doctors requested everyone to leave the room. My terrible situation was just above description.

Days passed and I wasn't talking to anyone, I just wanted to be alone, and I was waiting for the day to get back to Hungary to be away from these curses. But how can my life just get any worse? How can life mess me up even more? My dad told me with pain that he won't be able to support my study in Hungary any longer, I can't describe myself at this very moment, it felt like being stabbed by a rusty knife, my life simply collapsed in front of my eyes. I asked for the reason of course and my dad explained that "the main sources of finance in Jordan started to decline; workers' remittances and foreign grants decreased after the oil prices collapsed and created several problems in the Jordanian economy. A fiscal deficit led to serious financial imbalances due to a rapid increase of the external debt servicing payment. In addition to that the dissolving between Jordan and Palestine in July 1988 and other political factors caused these imbalances that ended with a currency crisis, a large devaluation of the Jordanian dinar and a huge increase in the inflation rate during late 1988 and early 1989.

So my dad explained what was supposed to last me for 3 years was all consumed during the first year. And because of that he had no choice but to give me this news.

As much as it was painful, I had nothing to say, I just requested from him to let me go back and get my personal stuff and say my goodbyes to all and everyone I knew in Hungary, but he told me that it wouldn't be possible and that whatever stuff I had in there could be replaced.

After a few days of total depression and the feeling of having lost everything, my dad told me that I could be self-dependent if I took a Tour-guiding course at the Jordanian University in Amman, and since I know German and English and my Arabic was also well, I could be successful. At that point I would've done anything just to earn money and be self-dependent rather than having my dreams crushed every time I stand on my feet.

I started the course and studied "Ancient History and Religions" and continued studying it even after the course. During the 3 Months of this intense training we traveled the entire country from north to south and from east to west.

After the end of the course I passed the examination, both spoken and written with flying marks and got officially licensed by the Ministry of Tourism as a class "A" Tour-Guide for English and German speaking Tour Groups. With that I became the Youngest Licensed Tour Guide in the Kingdom of Jordan.

What and Irony once again, the country that I always wanted to escape from, the country that I got a culture shock from, the country where I lost my family in, the country where I got my heart shuttered, the country where my dreams got lost in, was the same country that I had to represent to all the visitors. Being a tour guide meant being an ambassador, and that wasn't an easy task at all for a 19 year old.

I started to work right after I got my license issued, but I kept reminding myself that this wasn't my path and that it was just temporary, I just wanted to be a normal University Student and build my life from that point on.

My first tour group was from Austria, when I got into the tour bus, the bus driver couldn't grasp the idea that I was the tour guide for the group seated in the bus; that's how young I was, he thought it was just a joke, and so I had to present my ID and I presented myself to the group. Even the group was surprised. There was like a lot of uncertainty in the air, and it was indeed a challenge. When I started explaining about the site with absolute confidence and in a native speaking language, all I could see was open mouths. At the end of the program the hesitant bus driver got the highest tip in his history of driving tourists. That was a turning point and my reputation started to spread.

After several months I had some savings and decided to add another language to my list, so, I applied for a summer language course at a University in Perpignan, south of France.

On one hand, it was an escape from Jordan and on the other hand it was also an opportunity to study abroad once again. After completing all the necessary requirements I flew to Paris on May 10, 1990. A great experience that started as early as I got out of the airport; no single human being spoke a single word of English. It took me about 20 minutes to explain to the taxi driver that I wanted a hotel that is close to the Eifel Tower. Eventually I got there, checked in and started to explore Paris on foot. Truly an amazing city, I walked and walked for hours, and my main stop was at the Eifel Tower. A guy with a camera approached me and spoke in French, didn't of course understand a word, then I tried speaking in English but with no luck, with German was the same outcome, and after about 10 minutes he asked in Arabic "Do you speak Arabic?" and I didn't really know if I should laugh or get mad!! I answered him with a yes, I wish I didn't though, because his Arabic was just worse than my French, I guess he was from Algeria and was speaking barbarian rather than Arabic. In the end, hand gestures were the best method to communicate, and

I took a picture at the Eifel Tower with his Polaroid Camera which cost me a few French Francs.

The next day I took the flight to Perpignan and went to the University. I really loved it from the very first moment I arrived. The registrar arranged for my accommodation with a French Family, that by itself made me feel revived and wished that my days would just be like that moment. Everything went so smooth, everything was so nicely organized, no obstacles or whatsoever.

After having been oriented and all documents arranged, the owner of the house where I will be living at, arrived to pick me up. He was so gentle, so nice and on top of that he was an officer at the Immigration Office in Perpignan, so my residency was done with the at most ease. Finally I could say I was lucky.

The family was great, a mom a dad, 2 sons and a daughter; they always spoke in French with me and told me to get used to it, and only if I was totally stuck to speak in English. So whatever I was learning during class I was applying it on the family, they helped me so much and treated me as one of them, I never felt as a foreigner or an outsider. They taught me to love French cuisine, they taught me to enjoy food, they taught me to eat blue cheese and above all, they helped me learn French and love the language.

The University itself was awesome; it had foreign students from different parts of the world, from Finland, Sweden, Italy, USA, and many other countries. We all became friends and exchanged phone numbers and addresses.

In France I learned to enjoy beer after playing table tennis, I also had my first Casino experience and played Roulette for the first time in my life. I tried to learn about all and everything.

At the end of the Language Course I received my Diploma in French Language and Civilization.

July 1990, I had no choice but to return to Jordan once again; another pain fell on me to leave France where everything went so great and where I got to know a whole bunch of very nice people. But that was simply the story of my life; nothing that I liked and loved did last. And I have no idea why? On the airplane I met a very nice Palestinian family who told me whole heartedly to contact them if ever I will be able to come to Chicago; they were American citizens and resided in the USA for a long time. Somehow, this was comforting for me, despite that I had no plans to be in the USA.

And here the story goes on; I barely arrived back to Jordan to continue with my Tourism work, another political situation had to screw me up once again, the cold war of the first gulf war started during that period, tourists started to cancel their trips to Jordan due to its proximity to the region, and this was basically the end of tourism for that year. How much more bad luck can happen to a person? I then requested from my mom to help me out to go back to Hungary, I knew that my dad would be totally against it, and he won't support it. Probably I was selfish at that point, but whatever it was I just couldn't stand the thought to be in Jordan with no work and surrounded by problems and misery.

A week before classes started for the second year, I flew back to Hungary, and I just couldn't accept the fact that I was not going to continue with my studies, so I decided to speak it over with the registrar explaining why I missed a year in the first place and the current political situation in the Middle East. Whatever I explained was taken into consideration and I was allowed to continue with my second year with no payment under the condition that I have to make the first semester's payment before the end of the last final exam, I was OK with it because I was hopeful that a miracle might happen and that my dad or even my mom could help out somehow. The amount that my mom gave was basically survival money and in order for me to last longer in Hungary I stayed with some friends instead of being in my old apartment.

I really studied with passion despite that my hopes for a miracle to happen started to fade away, yet I wanted to be optimistic. I made it to the first set of examinations and took the first 2 exams. Despite that I made so well in these exams, I couldn't fool myself any longer and just surrendered and stopped. Maybe I should've done so from the start, but I just refused to accept the bitter facts.

Since I stopped and was no longer attending the rest of the exams, I just stayed in the house until my friends finished their exams. Then I decided to try my luck and apply for a Visa to the United States; and so it was; I went with my friends to Budapest. We had a really good time and after eating, I listened to a song named "Listen to my heart "by Roxette, after that it was time for my interview at the American Embassy in Budapest. I guess life wanted to smile on my face for a bit and I was so happy despite of all my built up sadness. I was granted a One Year Multiple Entry to the United States.

My friends in Hungary were extremely happy for me and they surprised me big time when they handed me an envelope that contained a 1,000 US Dollars as a gift from them.

Once again, I had to return to Jordan first, as it was always the point of departure to any new destination. My family already got used to me and to my constant running away of being around them for too long. They knew it had nothing to do with love, they knew that I love them very much, but they also knew that I could never forget nor forgive what they have done to me and my sisters, by getting us out from home, the country of our birth.

I decided to fly to Chicago for two reasons, the Palestinian Family that I met on the airplane on my way back from France to Jordan, and my friend and study mate at the University in Perpignan. I called her up prior to my booking to see if she would be willing to help me out once I arrive. She was very happy and told me that I was very welcome. And so the arrangements were made.

Two days before my departure to the USA I had very terrible stomachaches and had to see a doctor, so he gave me some medication and told me that it should solve the problem. I took the medication religiously as he explained and made sure not to leave them behind.

December 08, 1990 I first flew to New York and had an overnight there and the next day the hotel bus drove us to the airport to continue the flight to Chicago, while I was still on the bus, I felt severe pain in my neck and back muscles, I tried to ignore it as much as I could, but the pain was stronger than me. I really gathered my strength, got out of the bus, took my luggage and entered the airport, and here was my grand finale, I fell on the floor from the severe pain, wherein, my muscles cramped so hard that it twisted my back to one side and my neck to the opposite, the strangest most horrifying feeling I've ever had, I thought that I am dying on my first daylight in the USA, people were just watching, and as it seemed, no one dared to do anything. Suddenly the police arrived and started to question me, but I was in so much pain that I barely could answer; they took me to JFK Hospital/Medical Center. I had to fill out some forms which I did with at most difficulty, then I was asked if I had money, at that point I didn't care if all my 1,000 US Dollars would be taken, I just wanted a treatment, it felt like I am being split in half and my head was about to fall off my shoulders.

I was finally seen by a doctor, and when he saw that I was born in Germany he asked me in German if I was still able to speak the language, I answered him back in German "Please help me" and then he asked me if I was taking any medication, I took out the medicine that I was taking for my stomach, he shook his head and said your problem is solved, he gave me an injection and prescribed me some medication and asked me to stop the medicine that I was taking, since it was the cause of everything I've been through.

The doctor was so nice and let me stay for 30 minutes to make sure I was OK, and indeed my muscles relaxed and the pain faded away, it was an unforgettable experience that made me determined to become one day an American Citizen, I felt the total belongingness to this country despite that it was my very first entry. It was such a strange feeling and a very strange thought, yet totally genuine.

I was still able to catch my flight and arrived at Chicago on time, but my friend wasn't there at the airport, so I got furious since all that was left with me was only 860 US Dollars. I called her up and luckily, she answered, and apparently it was my mistake that I didn't give her the complete information, wherein, I missed to include which airport I will be landing at. It took her about an hour to arrive, but everything felt OK again. She took me to her house and introduced me to the people she was living with, and I just felt that I can easily fit in.

The next morning I went for a walk on my own, everything was so different here, I was comparing it to all the places I have been to, but it was incomparable. In the afternoon I called up the Palestinian family and told them that I was in Chicago. They invited me to visit them the next day, and I did. Unfortunately my aim of being helped to find a job was not accommodated. So it was a really rough and hard start, but I didn't mind it and kept going. A few days passed and everyone tried to help me, but it wasn't an easy process at all. Eventually I was able to find a place to stay at; I didn't want to be a burden to my friend and all the nice people I have known, it was an apartment with 4 rooms, 3 rooms were taken, and I got the 4th room. After paying the rent and the deposit I had a couple of hundred Dollars left with me to survive.

Despite the hard life I had, and the lack of survival funds and the unknown future, I had the feeling of belongingness to the USA; I applied for a Social Security number as I was advised to and kept searching for work. Day after day I was waking up early in the morning for my Job hunting. My funds started to evaporate, and my situation got extremely tight. Everything got even so much harder because the First Gulf War started, and the situation wasn't really pleasant at all.

On a very rainy evening I sat in front of the window and looked at the rain and my tears started to fall, I kept crying and crying until I was drained out. I was asking myself why all of this is happening to me? What wrong have I done in my 20 years of life? Why me? But it was just useless, as usual there were no answers.

The next day I received a phone call from my friend and thankfully she gave me some good news, there was a fast food restaurant that needed workers, I went to the address she gave me, which was pretty far, but I didn't really care.

I was accepted and told to start working in the evening; I was totally relieved but stressed at the same time, the money that I had left with me was enough to get me home only, I had no money to get me back to work in the evening.

When I reached my apartment, I went to the landlord who was of Greek origin, I explained to her my situation and requested from her to lend me a few Dollars that will last me for a week only. She was really polite and understanding and gave me what I requested.

At work I had to learn a lot and remember many names and techniques, I also had to do some heavy work as well; we were cleaning past midnight and dealing with grease, hot oil, and even entering the freezer when the weather was even freezing cold at that time.

The Manager and my co-workers loved me, so, that was a blessing by itself and it helped me tremendously to love my new job. After a week I got paid and I was able to fulfill my promise to my landlord and paid her back what I borrowed. Days passed and started to look brighter, and I started to stand on my feet. Afterwards I found a part time job at a Chinese restaurant and started to work as many hours as I possibly could handle. After 4 months I went to Truman College and inquired about studying, education was always my first and top priority. I was given an I-20 and I was advised to have my status changed to student, but there was no way of having it done from the USA, and since I was doing well at work, I planned on being a working student and be totally self-dependent, with that in mind I had to fly back to Jordan in order to change my Visa to a student Visa.

I was totally ready to have a life transformation, and in my mind, I was set that it would be the last time I have to fly back to Jordan. I requested a leave from work and explained that it wouldn't take long since I have all the documents ready. And indeed I flew back to Jordan in April 1991 with the intension not to exceed a week stay; Or so I thought.

On my second day of arrival I took myself to the US Embassy in Amman with all the necessary documents in order to have my Visa changed to a student Visa as Truman College in Chicago requested from me, I was really confident that I was on the right track and that I did everything correctly and as per law.

In seconds one person changed my life once again and threw me right back to Hell, made my life turn upside down and destroyed everything I have worked on so hard, everything I faced, handled and all the hardship I stood against went through thin air. The Consul and without a notice just stamped on my One Year Valid Visa with a one all capitalized word "CANCELED."

When I got home my face wasn't to be recognized and I just locked the door to my room and stayed there for the entire day with no food or drinks, my family tried to find out what was wrong with me, but the question should've been "what wasn't wrong?" I didn't reply and I didn't talk to a single soul.

Days went by, but I felt like a walking dead, and I used heavy smoking as a method of revenge, maybe I was just too naive and didn't know that I was just adding more troubles to myself. Day after day until June 1991 when my dad decided to get married since life was just too hard for him being alone and being responsible for my sisters and on top of that, me, the rebellion.

The wedding was set, and I did what I had to do and was happy for my dad, I danced and participated in that wedding as if I had no problems in life at all. I started fooling myself by believing that maybe if I go with the stream rather than going against it, my life will just get better. I did it because I was just too exhausted from having one disaster after another falling on me.

The woman that my dad got married to was really nice and we truly loved her, she didn't treat us as a stepmom, but as an elder sister, that helped us tremendously, especially on my sisters' part. That was necessary to have a bit of a break in life, most especially that my mom also got married prior to that, and to the same person she was accused with, what an Irony? So did that mean that there was really something going on? In that tone people tried to base their arguments and tried to convince me and my sisters, even the closest people related to us, what a rotten society?! The only reason my mom chose that way is to stop the running mouths that were talking about her, in such a society people can't say a word anymore if there is a legal contract binding two people together. The more I hated being in such an environment, everything has to be justified; everything has to be done according to traits and culture, why? Where is the freedom of choice? Why do we have to please people on our own expense?

My method of going with the stream was simply useless, no method worked for me, as if a curse was put on me from the time I was born, and what made this such a believable thought for me, was when I fell in love once again, it was so sudden and so unplanned. In fact how can you plan love? It just happens when you let your heart free, despite that I never forgot about my Angel and never stopped loving her, but she was no longer mine and no longer in Jordan even, she moved to Jerusalem and had been staying there ever since.

Two months after my dad got married; I got surprised one day with some visitors in the house, a pretty smiley green eyed young sweetheart whom I've never seen before, so I asked my dad's wife secretly who she was? She smiled and said, "that's my sister". With a sigh I entered my room and started thinking, what's going on? Shall I really believe that life may have some joy for me? Am I even allowed to be happy? My thoughts ended nowhere, so I decided to stop worrying and just go with the flow; whatever is meant to be, will be, and there's no escape from destiny. On the other hand I didn't even know whether this pretty girl will even be interested. So why rush things? I left my room and started talking to the people in the house until it was evening,

We all had a nice dinner together, and later at night my dad and his wife went to sleep, my sisters did the same and so I was alone with this sweetheart, the perfect opportunity to talk and get to know her, she was as I named her, a real "sweetheart", smart, ambitious and really understanding. We were talking until 4 in the morning as if we knew each other since ages. It really felt great to finally communicate with someone who was kind of different.

The feeling was mutual, we liked each other and this liking developed quickly into a secret relationship, since the culture again doesn't allow it, an issue that had to follow me around every corner while in the Middle East; and in order for this relationship to continue and in order for it to be blessed, and in order for me not to fall into the same drama as before with my Angel, I had to make a very bold move. The one and only choice that I had available if I wanted the relationship to prosper, the only choice acceptable by community and culture, being engaged was the only way out.

A 21 year old young man who went through so much in such a short time were none of his wounds have actually healed decides to get engaged. Why? Because he had to follow the trends of the country which his parents chose for him without even thinking what the consequences could be. I was already falling for the society's demands that I always refused and ran away from. And so it happened, after going through the traditional way of asking her parents' permission and blessings, then family visits and invitations, I ended up being engaged. With this move I was able to visit her freely and vice versa, things were great, and we had lovely times together. I even started to believe that maybe that was my destiny to get married early and just become part of the community that I always run away from, for many moments I wanted to believe that. Then I started to live the thought by searching for a job in Jordan, since tourism was still totally dead, due to the after effect and crises of the first gulf war.

I ended up working in a bar at a 5 start hotel in Amman, again a weird thing to happen and an added on irony, an Islamic country with many values and traditions, trends that needed to be followed in order to be accepted, yet the only job that I could find was in a place that is totally against all these values. But what else could I've done? Ask my parents for pocket money to go out with my fiancé? Or just sit at home and say I can't do that because the culture despises it, and the religion forbids it? Wherever I looked at, I was simply screwed. My responsibility towards my fiancé, my will and belief of self-dependency on one side, and the culture, religion and society that I tried to convince myself foolishly to belong to, on the other side.

I heard many comments from many people, and I just ignored it, and whoever pushed it, I shut them up by a logic demand "if you don't like it, and if it bothers you that much, then simply pay me what I earn from my job and I'll sit at home"

Eventually after 4 months I got sick of many arrogant customers and just left work, that wasn't really a problem for me, but what happened shortly afterwards was; and shocked me so hard that it gave me a lesson in life about people and their cruelty; it gave me a lesson about things I never believed that they existed.

One day I visited my fiancé and had a great time with her, we were laughing and giggling like never before, it was such a lovely time that I wanted to see her as soon as possible again. It took me just a couple of days and I was back again, but this time she was different, she was washing clothes by the time I entered the house, and she had a really long face, so I asked her what was wrong with her? But she just answered and in a very strange tone: "nothing", so I thought maybe she needed her space, and I didn't push it. I excused myself and told her to call me whenever she feels like it; and left.

I really didn't think of anything bad, people can have their mood swings and tantrums, and that's what I thought was the case, but surprisingly it wasn't. Almost midnight of the same day the phone rang, and my dad's wife answered it, her face couldn't be translated and after she hang up she asked me "did anything happen between you and your fiancé today?" so I told her that I even barely saw her and left due to her mood or whatever it was, and asked why? What was the midnight call all about? I was still not grasping it, I was still not thinking of anything bad, but started to get worried with all of this. Suddenly my dad and his wife changed their clothes and just left the house by saying "your fiancé is in the hospital, stay home with your sisters and we will call you if we'll be late" they didn't even give me the chance to say a word and or even make a decision. I was not only worried at this point but puzzled, what was happening? Some information was surely skipped, some things were totally not right.

I waited on fire; I was burning already and couldn't calm down anymore. This situation continued until 4 A.M; that was the time my dad and his wife came home, but they didn't seem alright, nevertheless, I made them speak out, I had to know what in heaven's name was going on? Yet, probably not knowing, would have been a better option for me.

My fiancé was in a weird mind condition that escalated a few hours after I saw her last, she was scratching her face and hit her head against the walls, and she was shouting, crying and laughing at the same time. Her family took her to the hospital, but the doctors all agreed that her health and vital signs are all normal and that it's something beyond medical science. When I heard these words, my jaw was about to drop of disbelief, and I asked what was that even supposed to mean? My dad's wife started crying and hugged me tight, I still didn't get it, but I knew it's something really bad, something I haven't experienced nor encountered yet in my life.

A few hours later, I got dressed to go and check on my fiancé whom I was worried sick about, but another surprise was just around the corner for me, I was not allowed to go there, so I stood with the most puzzled face in front of my dad and his wife wondering why the hell not? They told me that it will just aggravate the situation and that her condition was getting worse, if my name was being mentioned she became hyper crazy and wild, how much more if she sees me? I was listening to all these words and my heart was being smashed. I truly didn't know what to feel anymore. And all I wanted was to be of help, I wanted her to be OK and to get well. But the question was how? I didn't even know what was really wrong with her. And I wasn't even supposed to see her. With all of that I was totally helpless and clueless.

Another day passed and the situation got worse, her condition was indescribable, sunken eyes, scratched face, self-talking and shouting, even the voice has changed. I couldn't take the news any longer and had to see all of that with my own eyes, and I just wish that I didn't, it was extremely terrible, and the picture remains imprinted in my brain that could never be erased.

After I saw all of that from a different room without being noticed I decided that I had to do something, anything, just to make her better. And so I started asking her family and mine, and other people, whom to approach in cases like this? since scientifically she was a healthy human being. Surprises never stopped falling from the sky, how much was I just supposed to handle?

Apparently, I was dealing with something beyond my wildest imaginations; everybody said the same thing "Black Magic" As if everything in the past wasn't beyond my threshold, to be dealing now with insane things like this!!

I started to search for all the people who deal with these things, despite of my extreme refusal and disbelief, but the picture of my fiancé wouldn't leave my mind and kept me going. I traveled the entire Kingdom of Jordan searching for solutions and help, I met many of the so called "healers" and all of them basically mentioned the same, she has been targeted and big time affected by a power that was beyond their capacity to heal. Of course!! Everything has to be super complicated in my life and nothing ever comes the easy way.

With all the information I received I became more lost than I've ever been, the last healer I visited, told me that if I wanted to have this resolved I needed to find a Jewish healer to do that, because the "Black Magic" used was way too powerful. And that was a problem by itself again, because there were no Jews in Jordan. So, the healer gave me a name of a known person who was to be found in Syria, he explained that all I had to do was to find the Jewish Community in Damascus. With a big sigh and heavy heart I left. This was a really rough mission, something that was much more than I could handle. But I had to do it, not for myself but for the sake of this poor girl that was suffering from unknown reasons. The next day I went downtown and sold a gold necklace that I got as a present a few years back, in order for me to have enough money for a journey that was dangerous and unpredictable, a journey that dealt with powers beyond my beliefs and brain capacity.

I took my bag and asked my family to wish me good luck, since that was exactly what I needed, and the journey to the unknown started, was I scared? Oh Hell Yeah, I was for sure. I passed the borders and arrived in Damascus by Midday; I checked into a cheap motel, left my bag in the room and went out right away; there was no time to waste.

I took a taxi and told the driver to take me to the Jewish Community; the driver was actually wondering and asked me where exactly? And since I didn't have any address but a name, I was forced to explain; otherwise I would've ended up in an endless cycle. The driver was truly helpful and very accommodating and felt the terrible pain I was going through. So he took me to the area, and we started asking about the name, after about an hour we found the house, and I was so relieved and happy, but I was too fast to come to such a conclusion and feel that way. The neighbor came out and told us that he left for Switzerland about a month ago and that he doesn't know when he'll be back. At that moment I was just speechless, and I felt as if the entire universe was just against me, but what to do? Give up? I didn't learn from life to give up, and so I opted for the alternative since I already made this trip. I asked that neighbor if he knew anyone who was dealing in matters like his neighbor, since surely, they all knew. Kind enough he gave an address that was about 30 minutes away, and so it was. The driver took me to the new healer's address, however, another wonderful surprise; the man died some time ago. I was not only down and frustrated, but in a state of extreme anger towards my luck. The taxi driver was such a gentleman, he told me to cool down and that everything happens for a reason. Surprisingly, this young man who was probably in his late twenties offered to help despite that he didn't even know me; he took me to his family and introduced me to his mom and sisters, which is not a normal trend at all.

The mother heard my story and felt very sorry for me, and then she said that there was a much known woman close to the Jordanian border but on the Syrian side, she was so known, that even the Government asks for her help sometimes to solve certain mysteries. So I asked her to take me there and to extend her help despite that the location she mentioned was very far. And so it was, the next morning she and her son took me to that known lady healer. I waited for about an hour before it was my turn and then I entered the room.

She was an old lady with one eye, pretty scary, but I had no choice. She told me to sit down and gave me a round Arabian Coffee Cup that had no handles, this cup had just little coffee in it, barely a sip. Then she told me "This is not for you to drink, just put your hand over the cup." I did, then she put her hand over mine and closed her one eye and started speaking in a language I had no idea nor the slightest clue what it was.

Then she told me that my age was an odd number and my fiancé's was an even number, and that her eyes were green, this old lady started giving me information that were all totally correct. Then she gave the information which I was eagerly waiting, looking, and searching for

She said "You were invited to a lunch at your fiancé's home not long ago, and ate fish, whoever did this evil thing was someone close to her but I can't tell you who; the poison was put in the head part of the fish, you were meant to be the target and not her, but since you don't like the head part and she does, she got the poison of the "Black Magic". Then I asked for the solution and for her help, she shook her head and said "Son, this work is too powerful even for me, and it can only be resolved by your separation from her, she is forbidden unto you, someone wants her badly and used members of her family to achieve his goal. It's your choice son, either you'll be selfish and hold on unto her and the effect gets worse day after day, or you let go and she'll become better with time until the effect of this evil fades away.

Her word fell on me like a lightning falls on a tree and splits it in half, WOW, and just WOW, how can people do such evil? How can a person even accept on himself to be with someone through supernatural forces and not love? Why do people have an eye on something or somebody that doesn't belong to them? And even if it is humans' nature to envy, why go beyond the natural aspect of envy and do evil to get what they've envied? So many endless questions passed my mind and still pass to this very day.

The old woman stood up and told me, the solution is in your hand and no one else can do anything more than what I have told you, may God be with you and think wise.

I asked her how much I should pay her for the time and effort she exerted, but she refused to take any money and said, "your problem is so heavy on the heart and mind, that's more than a person could wish for" "I am sorry that I can't be of help more than my advice".

I thanked her and left, the driver and his mother were waiting for me and I told them what had happened, they were very surprised that the old woman didn't take any money, the more they were surprised with the story itself. On the way back to Damascus they stopped at a restaurant bought food and took me to their house, I was invited for lunch. Despite that I had no appetite at all, but I couldn't say no to this nice gesture.

After that I wanted to pay for the taxi service that was with me the entire time, but also them, they refused to take any money. They told me that I was a guest and that I could consider them as my family. So with everything that I have been through I was still blessed with having some people around me who helped me wholeheartedly.

The time has come, and I had to leave Syria and back to Jordan; the entire time I was thinking of the old woman's words, until I arrived at the house. I then shared my adventure with everybody at home, and all there was, just silence.

I made my decision and stepped over my heart for the sake of my fiancé's wellbeing, and that was the end of it, a few weeks later she started to feel better, regained her health and was pretty normal again. As for me I never saw her again.

A couple of months later, she got married to the guy who made this evil, and everything became as clear as a bright day. I just accepted the defeat and swallowed the pain and went on with my life.

Days passed and I was just going over my wounds and tried to heal whatever I could, I used suppression as my main strategy. At the same time I started studying about Astrology and its connection to letters and numbers and eventually its connection to human beings. But the topic was just too complicated and too complex for me, and so I just dropped the whole idea.

April 1992 my dad's wife brought a new member to the family, a baby girl, and I was asked to name her, without thinking or hesitation I named her after my first love "my Angel".

In the same month, Tourism started to pick up again and I was able to get back on track and make some decent money, rather than being surrounded with painful memories and being totally broke at the same time. But I felt the difference within myself; I was just down most of the time but hid it with a smile. It was good to work; in fact I exhausted myself working, so that I wouldn't have much time to think of anything. All I cared about was pleasing my tour groups and having a good time by pushing myself to suppress my thoughts of the past. I don't know if what I did was right? But I do know that it kept me going.

I was able to save some money during almost a years' work, and of course life has always something hidden for me, but this time it was quite different, I was stupid to fall for what I always rejected; trends and culture of the land. My family somehow planted in my head to go with the traditional way of getting married, this is done in a strange way wherein, families are being asked if they have single girls ready for marriage, then a visit by the females is arranged to get a first look and hunt for some information and background check, then another visit is being arranged where the guy and girl get to see each other and maybe talk for a bit, and based on that single meeting both parties have to give a reply. God, I was so against this wherein, I always believed that this method was just not right in my book. So how did I fall for it? What happened to me? Why did I say yes to the very idea that I rejected with passion? I was simply stupid and got dragged into a new life problem.

My main condition for my family was to find someone who was educated, at least to have her school years behind. And so, the hunt for a bride started.

I visited several families and saw several girls, but my choice fell on the last one I visited, I have no idea why? As if I was blinded, nevertheless it's still my total responsibility that I am carrying on my shoulders till this day.

Maybe the feedback I received was a major factor, I was told she finished school and that she was a great help for her mom in the house. And in my mind, I thought that would be somebody I could deal with; someone responsible.

There was an engagement period, but during that time for some strange reasons her family never let us be alone, and I didn't have much time anyway, so it didn't bother me much. I also didn't want to overthink or over analyze anymore, I even got myself into such an arrangement without having any feelings or whatsoever.

During the time that I wasn't seeing her due to my work and due to her family, I was receiving letters from her, and it appeared that she had a nice handwriting. That assured me that the information I got about her were correct. Days passed and a wedding date was set for June 1993. Honestly, I wasn't excited about it; I just wanted to bury myself in Jordan with no more thinking of going out, by having a family responsibility, I didn't think of love anymore cause all I got from love was pain, I didn't even think of studying either cause every time I did, I was just hit on my head. I think despite of my suppression technique and defense mechanism, I was having a depression, that's why I was throwing myself away like this.

In the morning of the wedding day I woke up with a severe headache and then it escalated to severe vomiting and diarrhea, I was taken to the hospital and got admitted right away. This was the second time I got admitted to a hospital after my birth, I guess God was sending me a sign, but I didn't understand it. Stupid me!!!

I stayed in the hospital for about 10 hours and was given strong medication to make me stand on my feet for that wedding. I wish I never stood again.

Even during the wedding there was a power outage, another sign that I didn't grasp, and in the end and just minutes before the bride should be driven to the house of the groom another problem arose, her family requested an amount for a dress that they bought for her. And that's when it hit me, I was so mad, disappointed, disgusted and finally totally insightful. I told my family to cancel everything and not to do it. It wasn't a matter of money but a matter of principal. And then I sited all the signs, but as if I was talking to walls of bricks, No one listened to me and they just said that I was just upset with everything that happened during the day. Why did I give in to what they said? Why didn't I just continue with what was in my head? Behind my back and without my knowledge the money was paid, and the bride arrived.

Alone in the house with a woman that I didn't love yet was my wife already, I didn't know what to do? I felt weak against the temptation and I convinced myself that maybe things will be OK. That is where I screwed myself up by being illogic, setting my brain aside and driven by my libido.

I really tried to ignore everything and I tried to live my days by fooling myself that everything was perfect, until one day when I took my bride out for a long walk, on the way we passed by the United Nation Building, and proudly I mentioned to her that in this building I applied for a job some time ago, yet to my surprise she didn't make a comment, so I asked her to read the sign on the building and was waiting for a reaction, but still nothing at all. Now I was furious and asked her what was wrong with her? Still there was no reaction! So I looked her in the eyes and asked her to tell me what was wrong? And here she sliced my throat with her words and the hidden truth; and informed me that she doesn't know how to read or write, that she was illiterate. I was in shock and couldn't believe what I heard. I really wished that the ground would open and swallow me. How in Heavens name can people cheat like that? All I knew is that people would cheat when they sell products, but not when it comes human beings. Was I really that naive? Or did I just anticipate the best in people?

In order for me not to make her feel bad, I told her that I will hire a private tutor and that it didn't matter how expensive it would be. We went home and spoke further about this topic, and I asked her who sent me the letters then when we were engaged? And it turned out that it was her sister. I was listening and my mind was exploding from anger knowing I got fooled. Nevertheless, I still gave it a try and told her to learn, learning and education are crucial and necessary. I also explained that I wasn't asking this for myself but for her own sake.

She promised she would, and I believed, but that wasn't the only problem, I discovered afterwards that she was messy and didn't even know how to cook. All the food I ate till that point was coming from my dad's house. I really couldn't take it anymore and just exploded. Even with that, they lied to me about!? What the heck?

I was also mad at my family because they aided her, and I was so left in the dark, it seemed to me that it was all planned to keep me in Jordan, they knew that I was struggling and that my thoughts were just to accept the facts and settle down where I didn't want to be. But was that really the right solution? I was miserable with this marriage; the fact that I was cheated kept hunting me.

One of my methods of survival was running away from the bitter facts, and every time I got the chance to go somewhere, I didn't think twice. In January of 1994 was one of these escapes; just days after my dads' wife delivered her second daughter, whom I also named; and this time it was the same name as my Angel's sister name. I think I was cloning my Angel's family into mine.

Anyway, I went to Israel this time. I visited some relatives and also visited my old love "my Angel" who resided with her family in Jerusalem. They knew about my misery and just tried to comfort me by telling me to be patient and that things will be alright. But how could they? Even my Angel was in a misery; her husband wasn't really a good man and was treating her badly. Yet I had my own problems to deal with and couldn't comfort anyone.

When I went back to Jordan, I still tried to make it work and just accept it all, but the same issues were continuously rising, nothing ever changed. When I decided to get a divorce, I simply couldn't because she was pregnant already. I was teased by destiny and had to wait until my first child was born, a baby girl came to life on September 15, 1994.

Having a child at the age of 24 was a great feeling but living a life where you get in touch with the woman you live with, for the sole purpose of sex wasn't. There was no common ground between us. I still extended my patience though for the sake of my daughter, under the condition that this woman starts taking contraceptives; since it was obvious that this relationship was nothing more than a legal, blessed by the community sexual relationship.

But again I admit that it was my fault to even believe that she would follow an agreement, I just anticipated that since there was a child already that she would actually change and become a productive human being. I wanted to believe that people can change when they set their minds to it. In general that would be true I believe, but with her I was totally wrong.

In January 1995 I went once more to Israel, and this was my first time to visit Eilat, a beautiful city in the far south. To my surprise I was the first Jordanian passport holder who visited the hotel that I was in, and as a gift from the hotel they upgraded my room to a suite with no extra charge. To me this was an iconic visit since it occurred just two month and a few days from the signing of the peace treaty between Israel and Jordan. During that trip I met with a girl from Switzerland whom I've known during one of my tours in Jordan. I didn't feel guilty at all because I just didn't believe, nor did I acknowledge that I was in a relationship, or in other words married.

Just a few months after my visit to Israel I left for Italy, every time I saved some money, I spent it on running away, having some good time or rather making myself believe to have some good time. I didn't mind it though; my dreams were lost anyway, and I was just living day by day with no ambition anymore. I visited Rome, the Vatican, Pisa and finally Florence where my Italian girl-friend lived, we became best friends when we studied in France. I truly spent a wonderful time with her and her family, and the best part was the eating of Italian pasta.

But as usual, every escape from Jordan was faced with another return, and so I worked very hard and tried even harder to be away from the house as much as I could. This worked for almost a year until I found out that she was pregnant again, I flared up from anger and shouted as if it was my last day on earth, and how I wish it was. I was fooled once again, she did it and got me big time. She wasn't taking the contraceptives and kept lying to my face about it. I was determined that this was the end and spoke it over again with my family, yet they stood against me and strongly even, to the extent that my dad told me straight up, if I was to do it, I no longer would be his son. That was a harsh slap on my face. For one, another pregnancy that I made sure it wouldn't happen, yet it happened, and a threatening father who had no clue what I have been going through.

I made many mistakes in my life; but listening to my family and caring for their opinion at that stage was one of my biggest mistakes. What was I supposed to do? I was so lost, so unhappy and on top of that I had to continue living with a woman that I couldn't even stand. If it wasn't for the humans need to have sex, I wouldn't have known how to pass the days. It may sound mean even to me, but it is still the absolute truth.

The days passed as usual, and my second child came to life on March 17, 1996. A boy this time, yet when he was born, I wasn't even in the city and didn't see him until he was a week old. The good thing about my work was the staying out and away for days.

I didn't have the power nor the will to make things work anymore; I was upset with my dads' threat and my fake marriage, this wasn't a life, yet I had to live it. I tried my best not to even touch her anymore; I tried not to be at home anymore and I even took as much work as I could to be away.

And again a new travel was planned in July of 1996 and this time it was to Istanbul-Turkey, I probably wanted to deliver a message to my dad, that even with my fake marriage and the kids I have, he couldn't keep me in a place that I didn't want to be at. I also wanted to deliver that his unfair stand against my divorce couldn't stop me from doing what was right for me. I just wish I had the guts and would've taken the option of divorce despite my dads' threat of disowning me.

Nevertheless, I spent much money going in and out of Jordan and finally decided that it was time to put my brains back into function. That decision came after my trip to Lebanon in September 1997. I applied through an agent in Jordan to have distance learning and to study Political Science at the University of Lebanon. I only needed to attend the University during the examination period. And so I started and studied with passion, since education was always my dream. When the time came for the first semester's exams the Lebanese Embassy refused to give me a Visa despite of my student status, so again another dream crashed for no reason. I didn't consider the time spent on studying as a waste, but as an added knowledge, it seemed that it wasn't my time yet to get my degree. It hurt much, nevertheless, most especially that when I went there as a tourist, I was given a Visa, but when it was time for fulfilling an education dream it was rejected. What a strange life we are living!!!

I barely caught my breath from not being allowed to attend my exams to a car accident my dad got injured at, he hit his head but was alright, or so we thought. Nothing really was noticed with him until a couple of months later. All of a sudden, my dad collapsed and was admitted to the hospital; apparently that car accident he had caused a part of his brain to bleed, the blood clot was becoming bigger and bigger and was pressuring the brain. He had to undergo immediate brain surgery and stayed in the ICU for quite some time. After the surgery my dad forgot all of us and couldn't remember a single thing. On top of that he became half paralyzed as well. This situation was so terrible and nerve racking. How much more does a person have to face in life before he gives up? This situation stayed like this for 2 months until a miracle happened, and my dad regained full memory, speech and movement after almost 5 months. Truly God's mercy was with my dad and with us, to get out of this terrible situation.

However, the usual mess kept hunting me on a daily basis and I just had to swallow it all and wait, waiting and patience were all I had. And again it was time to run; I had some money saved which I used for my trip to Germany and Austria in July of 1998. I was reunited with my childhood friends and had an amazing time. I just ignored my pain and tried to live the moment. We were laughing and giggling and just remembered all the kids' stuff we did back in the days. I felt alive again; I felt hope, love, joy, honesty and belongingness. Everything seemed so right and so normal.

It was so funny when we remembered what we did during our 2nd grade, I and my best friend and our female friend went to school almost every day together. One time it was snowing so hard during the night and in the morning, everything was so beautiful white especially with the sun shining on the white surface. On the way to school we had to walk many stairs down to the village and alongside the stairs were iron rails to hold unto, especially for the elderly people. While we were walking our female friend said "oh look the ice on the rails, it's so yummy, and it's like real ice cream" indeed the glance of the sun on the frozen ice on those rails looked so tempting. So me and my best friend got tempted and stuck our tongues out to lick the ice, and just imagine what happened to us poor kids? I and my best friend got stuck on the rails and our female friend was laughing her guts out, she left us and went to school, and we were stuck with our tongues out and crying. My friend was able to release himself first and then pulled me by force and freed me as well; both of our tongues were bleeding, so we went home. On top of that we got scolded by our parents and missed school. We were so mad at our female friend that we didn't talk to her for weeks. Recalling all these memories was just awesome.

After I spent almost 3 weeks in Germany I left for Austria and visited a family that was with me on one of my tours in Jordan. The family was very accommodating and nice, yet my major reason for going there was to meet with their daughter who actually fell in love with me while we were on tour. I didn't really know if I had any feelings at all, but I just wanted to see her. To my surprise it wasn't only the daughter, but also the mother was eyeing on me, and that was very embarrassing when I knew. The next morning I was in the house alone with the mother because the husband went to work, and the kids went for school. The mother made a nice breakfast and then invited me to swim in their swimming pool. So I went to the room and wore my trunks, but she was inside the pool already and totally naked. She then commented and said "really? You have a naked woman in the pool, and you will wear trunks?" I was speechless and didn't know how to react or what to say? She came out of the pool and took off my trunks and threw me in the pool. I really have no idea how I even could describe the weird feeling that I had. So to escape it I made myself as if I had swallowed water and started coughing and coughing and went out of the pool.

She brought me a towel and a glass of water and said "I am sorry I didn't mean to throw you in the pool like this, I just wanted you to have some fun" I in return said that it was OK, I just was unprepared and didn't see it coming. I was able to open a conversation and get her mind away of what she was thinking. Later that evening, I surprised them all that I had to leave urgently and said my goodbyes. I had to make an escape before the incident would be repeated.

I stayed in a hotel for the remaining days and enjoyed myself by touring around; since I knew that I will be back to the same mess again.

Indeed there was a return to Jordan, and for some unknown reasons I was fooled once again by my so called wife and I still blame myself about falling into this trap until this very day. She convinced me that she will change for the best and take care of the kids and herself. She mentioned that she'll be learning for the sake of the kids and asked me, begging with tears to give her one last chance. I think I am weak in front tears, and I also know for a fact that I didn't learn by then about the existence of Crocodile Tears. Nevertheless, I gave that chance for the sake of my children. Was it a Mistake? Yes, it was.

With a bit of luck I didn't stay for long, by November 1998 I accepted a Job offer from a Tourist Agency in Dubai-The United Arab Emirates, I started working as a tour guide after taking my full training there.

One day I received a phone call, and it was from the woman I had two kids from, the woman I had a new deal with, she informed me that she was pregnant again. Was it her fault? NO, it was mine and totally mine. So I didn't comment anymore, and I didn't get mad, since being mad wouldn't have helped me at all. On the contrary, I took this new deal into serious consideration and wanted to believe that she was serious as well. And to prove to her and to myself that I was not joking about this last chance I sent her a plane ticket to come to Dubai.

Probably it was a good thing that it happened that way, cause with this trip she made and for the first time in her life, I was able to determine that there was no chance in Hell to continue with this fake marriage. She told me straight to my face that I wouldn't dare to leave her with my dads' threat of disowning me, and on top of that having three kids. I didn't argue and I didn't say anything. I let her enjoy her week stay and drove her to the airport in the end.

I finished my contract in Dubai and left for Jordan with an absolute determination to correct the long lasted mistake. I spoke with my father and I totally was ready to be disowned. I was drowning more and more, and that was just way too much for me to handle.

I discovered then that even my family was suffering from her actions, and they just tried to have patience with her for the sake of the kids. But they only believed me after they got a dose of what I have been taking for a really long time. Despite that I love my family very much, but I didn't feel sorry at all, simply because they just brought it up on themselves.

The actual separation started, and I filed for a divorce right the moment I got the chance to. The process was very bitter as I do believe are most of the divorce cases. Nevertheless it had to be done and a long time ago even.

And as life always promised me with some real hard time another problem had to fall on my head, but this time of a totally different type. While I was waiting for the divorce process, I got myself busy with a tour group, I had a 7 day tour program and as most programs, they end in the far south at a city called Aqaba, my group arrived but I didn't, what happened was and still is a mystery and the pain never went away. On the way to Aqaba we passed through a valley called "Wadi Araba" and halfway through we stopped for a smoke and to exercise the feet from the long sitting in the bus. I was explaining about the extreme proximity between the Jordanian borders and Israel and how great it was that peace was achieved, suddenly and out of the blue an old military jeep arrived and stopped in front of the bus, two soldiers stepped down and asked who the tour guide was; so I answered them, and they asked me what I was doing there? Pretty stupid question yet I answered them, but for some reason they didn't like it and told me that I have to go with them to their superior without indicating the reasons. So I requested the driver to take the group to Aqaba and I went with these soldiers to the unknown. I was beaten black and blue for no damn reason and their superior was telling the soldiers to stay away from my face. I really got terrified because I didn't know why? What wrong have I possibly done to deserve this? Am I not an ambassador who fulfilled his duty to the fullest?

I couldn't tell anyone about this bad incident not even my own family and I kept this dark day as my secret. This was my very last day I worked as a tour guide; I decided that I didn't have to deal with this kind of crap.

At this point of my life I was totally fed up already, nothing went right, and when it did it was just temporary, as if life was just giving me morphine injections.

Around December of 1999 I applied for a Visa at the American Embassy in Amman-Jordan and was granted a very limited time and restricted Visa; I had to take the chance and flew back to the USA on February 01, 2000.

As always, every new start is devastating and extremely hard, especially when no one is around to help out. I first flew to Chicago and stayed there for a few days, and then I remembered that I had a work friend from Jordan who resided in Texas, I called him up and explained my situation, thankfully he agreed to accommodate me for some time and indeed I booked the cheapest ticket and flew to Dallas.

This friend was nice enough and picked me up from the airport and took me to his apartment which was pretty small, but at least I had a place to stay at. I didn't mind sleeping in the living room on the couch, something was better than nothing.

A few days passed and I was just getting adjusted to the place, then I decided to make use of my stay and started looking for a Job, which wasn't easy at all. I was really scared of the thought having to return to Jordan, the beating that I got for no reason made me realize that I have no future there. Applying for an asylum crossed my mind but I didn't have the funds. Everything was just upside down.

I walked for more than 2 hours to reach the DMV to take my driving test, my friend was working, and I couldn't be dependent on him, I had to do everything I could to stand on my feet and not to return to Jordan. That fear kept hunting me day after day.

After almost 2 months I was able to find a job at a convenient store and gas station, I rented an apartment close by so that I had not to worry about any transportation. I started to work at their kitchen and arrange the shelves of the store. The starting per hour rate was pretty low, but when a person doesn't have many choices, anything would do.

A few months passed and I was able to save some money, despite that my pay wasn't that good but I tried my best. I impressed my employer with the way I work, I learned everything in a very short span of time and moved afterwards to run the cash register. Before I knew it, I became the manager of the store and my pay increased to $10/hour. However, with every position comes a bigger responsibility, I had to put in extra time, be early at the store and leave late.

One early morning I came to the store, prepared coffee and opened the door, just minutes later a customer came in, grabbed a coffee and put on the table a pile of 100$ bills, he said with a low tone "these are $5,000, it's yours everyday if you work with me" I understood right away that it was something really bad, and politely I apologized and refused the offer. I am proud of myself that I didn't get tempted despite of my extreme need for money. That man never came back either, which was a blessing by itself.

Working was basically all I did; I had no chance and no time doing anything else until I met a new co-worker, who was very nice and very helpful, we became friends' very quick and started going out for coffee and breakfasts and sometimes for late dinners. He was 10 years older than me; but it was alright, since I never believed that friends should be of the same age group. After some time I also met his brother who also was a real gentleman. This brother helped me a lot and cosigned me to buy a new car; my very first car was a Maroon Ford Focus, this move made me more free and able to explore the city. However, what was lacking was a woman in my life, but since I had no luck so far with any of my previous relationships, I was very hesitant.

One day I decided to give it a shot, and since I didn't have that much time due to work, I applied for a match making agency, it really cost me a lot, but I just wanted to feel life again.

I had several dates but none of them worked out for me until my last date. When I spoke with her on the phone, I was already excited meeting her. And that's what happened, I picked her up from where she lived and went out with her on a very simple date, we had coffee and talked about general things and had a bit of laughs. Despite that I wanted to be with an American, yet she was an Asian from the Philippines, I didn't really mind it, since I had a good time with her and she seemed to be a really lovely girl. When I drove her back to the house she used to live in, I asked her when I could see her again. She replied with a smile "Why? Are we going to have another date?" I smiled back and told her that I will call her.

We exchanged phone calls and had nice conversations and laughs and it stayed that way until we met again. This time I took her to a park close to where I used to live, and we sat on the grass facing some water that was river-like. Just minutes after we sat, I had the guts to lie down on her lab; however, she was stiff like a rock, she didn't anticipate my move and I didn't mind it. I was just happy being with her. I looked her in the eyes and told her that I really liked her and that I haven't had this feeling in a long time. She just smiled and told me "you don't even know me yet" I agreed but answered her back with a statement "sometimes we live with people for so many years and think that we know them, yet we get so surprised when we find out that we were very wrong" this statement of mine made me serious at that moment and l kind of lost the momentum. As much as I tried to run away with my thoughts from the past, but they just kept hunting me.

Later that evening she called me up and told me that maybe it won't work out between us, I was surprised with her assumption and asked why? Apparently, she had an issue with my religion. I explained to her that these matters shouldn't even been brought up, because what matters is what a person really is, his/her character and attributes. Color, Race and Religion are never an indicator of what a person really is. I was disappointed with her but still didn't want to give up; I had this warm feeling for her and wanted to see where it might lead to.

She stopped calling me afterwards and even stopped answering my calls, and so I stopped trying but didn't forget about her. One night I went out clubbing with some friends and to my huge surprise I saw her there with some really tall guy; I was wondering and asking myself "of all the clubs in the city and of all the days and weeks that passed, why see her at this place and time?" So I decided not to let her see me and just leave, wherein, she did the same, she apparently saw me as well and decided to leave without me seeing her, and when destiny decides, we can't just escape it, we bumped against each other and face to face. Both of us were in a state of disbelief and tried to make a polite escape from this destiny meeting. She smiled and I smiled back and then we went on our respective ways. My heart was truly beating, and I just couldn't hold myself from not calling her. For some reason she answered her phone, as if she also understood the message of destiny. I asked her how she was, and that I was happy seeing her earlier. She told me that she saw me and decided to leave because she didn't want to have an encounter with me since she hasn't returned any of my calls the past few weeks. We spoke for about 15 minutes and it seemed to me that cupid played a role here.

But life always promised me with surprises, the good and the bad, and another unexpected surprise came my way, when I tried calling her the next day, she was out of coverage area, so I kept trying and trying for days, but it was always the same. There was no news from her, she just disappeared. So about a month after her disappearance I drove to the house where she resided at and asked about her, her friends whom she used to live with told me that she flew back to the Philippines. I then requested her phone number, but they really gave me a hard time about it; but with my perseverance they gave me the house number stating that they didn't know her private number. I thanked the girls and left.

In the evening I called the house number which I was given, and some girl answered the phone, so when I asked about the queen, this girl started to laugh and told me that she was her sister. She told me that she was working at their Pharmacy and gave me her number. I thanked her, hang up and called the new number. It was her; my heart once again beat so fast when I heard her voice. She on the other hand when she heard my voice didn't really believe that I was calling her and asked me where I was? And out of humor I told her that I was just nearby and behind the tree without even knowing if there were any trees in the area, I just gave it a shot; I even made it more exciting when I stated that there was a white car nearby as well. Later on I found out that she really bought it and stood up slowly looking around searching for me. Despite that it was a long distance call I stayed on the phone with her for almost half an hour. At the end of the phone call I told her straight up that I had strong feelings for her. I knew right then and there that I wanted to have a future with her despite of all the possible obstacles.

Speaking of obstacles, I always had those; my life never went the way I wanted and when it did something had to come my way to destroy everything that I have built or was still building. I received a phone call on January 07 of 2002, but this call was like no other. It was from the FBI who made an appointment to visit me at home for the next day at 1 PM. It was a terrible night for me, my thoughts were wandering in the unknown world, and the minutes were passing as if they were years until it was finally 1 PM, and on the dot the doorbell rang. Two Gentlemen were on the door, One FBI agent and an Immigration Agent. Of course I invited them in. The visit was a procedure taken by the FBI after the sad and terrible 9/11 attacks. They asked me about every single detail, and I answered them with all honesty, I was so honest that they were surprised about my answers. Of course one major question arose, "why didn't you try to change your status instead of overstaying?" so I answered "I had two options, the first was to get married to an American Citizen, but I wouldn't do that if I didn't fall in love, I would never do such an act for some papers. Marriage to me is sacred and I believe in that wholeheartedly. The second option was to apply for "political asylum", yet there was a problem with that as well, the attorney's cost was just too high for me to afford it, and my case was weak anyway because I had no proves or whatsoever to the bad beating that I got from some army personnel in Jordan when I was with the tour group explaining about the peace achievement between Jordan and Israel. Furthermore, the relationship between the USA and Jordan is great. So what was I supposed to do? My responsibility towards my family and my fear of returning to Jordan made me stay. I had no other options. I further stated that I made no crime by trying to be safe and being responsible for my family. But I also know that I broke the law by overstaying despite of the factors that made me do it.

At the end the FBI agent told me that they were aware of my answers and that I answered with the at most confidence, then he added that the FBI had nothing against me, but he would leave the rest to the Immigration Officer. Here the situation was different; the agent told me that he felt me and that it's hard to be in my shoes, but I made a mistake by overstaying regardless of the circumstances. Then he told me that because of my honesty he will not take me in, however, I will be receiving a letter within 2 weeks with a court hearing where my case will be decided in courts. In the meantime I could work on my political asylum case if ever I wanted to pursue with it. He took my passport and gave me a piece of paper which proved that my passport was taken. The two gentlemen left, and I was lost, totally lost.

About two weeks later I received the letter from the Immigration stating that there would be a court hearing at an "unscheduled date", there was a case number printed out with a phone number to follow up on the case. Surprisingly, a writer from the Metropolitan Newspaper "The Dallas Morning News" called me up two days later and conducted an interview with me over the phone, then he requested to have my case published in his paper. And so it was; on January 28, 2002, the following article was published:

"FBI still seeking Mideast men.

Interviews incomplete in N. Texas

Ahmad Khalaf admits that he came to Dallas 18 months ago by telling a small lie and breaking a couple of immigration laws.

The 31-year-old citizen of Jordan said he persuaded the U.S Embassy there to grant him a short-term visitor visa even though he secretly planned to stay illegally in Dallas and make money to support family back home.

Mr. Khalaf said his plan was successful, and he was working at a local convenience store gas station. Then federal agents from the FBI and the Immigration and Naturalization Service knocked on his door last month.

His name, they said had turned up on a list of 5,000 Middle Eastern men, including 360 in the federal Northern District of Texas, who are being systematically questioned by the FBI. The U.S Justice Department operation, billed as an effort to root out hidden terrorists and learn about al-Qaeda recruiting efforts that many have targeted young men, was supposed to have ended by the New Year.

Officials say North Texas is among a handful of regions that have delayed the program's end, partly because of the effort required to find the 360 people.

The operation, however, seems to be turning up far more immigration law violators such as Mr. Khalaf than important terror-related intelligence, federal officials said.

The Dallas area has one of the nation's largest concentrations of immigrants from the Middle East –an estimated 138,000 people.

Federal authorities sometimes with assistance from local police, have concentrated their efforts to locate the 360 young men in communities in Richardson and Arlington, the locations of large mosques.

Dallas FBI Special Agent in Charge Danny Deffenbaugh said his staff has been able to interview only about half of the 360 men in North Texas since U.S Attorney General John Ashcroft ordered the operation. One reason the effort has not moved faster, he said, is that finding immigrants who typically move frequently within such a large population – perhaps more frequently since Sept. 11- has proved difficult.

Agents have been forced to find the men by checking information in INS visa records, which is time consuming.

For all the efforts expended interviewing the men in the Dallas area, Agent Deffenbaugh said, only two individuals seemed to warrant a return visit related to terrorism.

"They may be in a position to have known some things that we would have investigative interest in," he said, declining to elaborate.

Mr. Khalaf said he has agreed to return to Jordan or face jail in Dallas and eventual deportation.

"Being honest is a crime nowadays, I guess," he said. "I have nothing to hide. I did nothing wrong except for overstaying, and I overstayed to support my family, and that's not a crime."

Justice Department officials said they have been instructed not to publicly discuss what intelligence value the program has yielded nationally, at least until it is declared over.

Bryan Sierra, a Justice Department spokesman in Washington D.C., said the program would have been wrapped up if not for "a few areas that needed more time than others, areas with higher concentrations of people."

He said the program had proved to be more than merely a policing operation by the INS.

"Some information has proved to be useful in anti-terrorism efforts, overall," Mr. Sierra said.

The program has drawn a variety of critics, including civil rights advocators who say the government is illegally profiling suspects on race.

One Dallas immigration lawyer who has provided advice to a number of men who have been approached by federal agents said the operation is little more than a thinly disguised effort to clear out illegal immigrants from Middle Eastern countries.

Karen Pennington said the operation unfairly targets one demographic group on the basis of race, leaving other ethnic groups known for illegal U.S. presence in high numbers unscathed.

"It seems to be a pretext to get them out on immigration charges", she said. " They're looking for overstays to get rid of them."

Anne Estrada, head of the Dallas district of the INS, said her agency has taken a direct role in the operation for good reason. INS database are an obvious starting point to determine a person's immigration status and track down violators using personal information provided in visa applications. But she said the process can be arduous.

Once immigration status appears to be outdated, she said, INS is obligated to help find the violator and enforce the law. She said the 15 Middle Eastern men in her jurisdiction have been rousted in this way.

"You need that personal interview," she said.

Ms. Pennington, the immigration lawyer, said she has heard no complaints from any of those targeted about mistreatment by federal agents. She said her clients have described the agents as "polite, nice, professional."

Agent Deffenbaugh has ordered his staff to go easy on those being questioned to avoid provoking a backlash. Everyone so far has cooperated in a way that has satisfied the questioners, although three men had to be arrested on immigration charges, he said."

This published article was quite all right, yet, I had no chance to correct a few mistakes that were to be found between the lines, I never persuaded the Embassy nor had the plan to overstay in the USA, I was hoping to find a legal way to stay in the country that I always considered as being my home since the first time I landed there. I never had such a strong feeling about any place other than Germany and Israel.

Shortly after, I received a phone call from my family informing me that my best friend in Jordan whom I've become friends with since 1991, an amazing guy who was born and raised in Venezuela; passed away in a terrible car accident. The impact of his death was tremendous yet, I didn't know how to react to it, I felt as if I was betrayed, that I was left alone on the face of this earth. When you lose someone who's so close to you, you feel all different kinds of feelings. I had to overcome that chapter of my life by suppressing my thoughts. `

Despite what I've been through, and all that mess that fell on my head, despite my fear of the unknown, I kept calling my queen in the Philippines every time I got the chance to, until one day when I called, she wasn't there anymore, and I was told by her family that she left the Philippines. Once again, I lost her and didn't know where she was, I really don't know why I accepted that on myself. Shouldn't that have been a sign for me to just turn my back? Now I was without my passport and without my queen and nothing seemed right anymore. Well, the real question is: "when did it seem right?"

I haven't heard from her anymore for several months and I also haven't heard anything from the INS nor from the FBI. I never got a hearing date either. I was almost on a nervous breakdown; everything was just simply upside down. Every time I called the INS number that was provided in the letter that I received, an automated system requested me to enter the case number, and when I did so, the response was always the same "No Case Found" Just imagine a situation like mine!! I shouldn't stay according to the law, and I can't leave either because of the law, I didn't know what I was supposed to do. And so I tried to adapt to my new situation of being clueless and lost and tried not to think about it anymore. I lived my days, day by day, and was waiting for the grand finale.

One evening my phone rang, it was a California number. This time it was my turn to be surprised; her voice flew through my veins. I didn't know if I should've been mad or happy, I didn't know what to say, act or react. But the words that came out of my mouth were "I Missed You".

We spoke and spoke and made up for the lost time. This phone call of hers was a total transformation in our relationship. From that point on we called each other on a daily basis. The greatest phone call was on September 07, 2002, when she finally admitted her feelings and said it loud and clear "I Love You".

At that time I felt that life was giving me a chance again and I forgot the daily pain that I had from my delightful situation. I was looking forward to anything that would make me happy again as when I was a child, a feeling that I was craving for. What's so unfair about life is that we can't see what's hidden for us, we make certain choices, fight for what we want, and suffer the consequences of the momentum without even knowing what tomorrow has in its folds for us.

We agreed that she will leave California and come to Dallas so that we could start our relationship on solid grounds, and not just over the phone. And so it happened, by October 2002 she came to Dallas and I was very happy picking her up from the airport. For the first time, I embraced her and felt life, I felt happiness and joy. Once she got inside my car, I also got my first romantic kiss. No matter how much I describe the happiness I was in, I just wouldn't be able to give it any just. How life can be so contradicting?! I was in the world of the unknown; my heart bled from not knowing what would happen to me, yet I was very happy being in love again.

We were officially lovers at that point, but with an unknown path still. I drove her to her friends' house where she used to live before and made sure she was all right. The next day I visited her, and we watched our first movie together "A Walk to Remember" I had a great time with her. She made a simple Filipino dish called "Pancit Canton" and I ate as if I was in starvation. I think when a person is really in love everything tastes and feels so different.

But I knew deep inside myself that I wasn't secure; I had an ongoing issue that I didn't know what to do about? 9 Months passed already, and I had no scheduled hearing, I had no clue what was going on. So in order for me to have peace of mind and in order for me to start my new love with some sense of security, I decided to call the INS agent who took my passport. But instead of getting answers, I got more puzzled, the agent was no longer in service and I was really scared to ask further. With a huge, big sigh I hang up and my tears started falling. Do you know how hard it is to fight for survival, to fight for happiness, to fight for belongingness? The fear of having to return to Jordan was killing me every day; I just wanted to be in the USA and serve the country. With the thought of serving, I called up the FBI agent and reminded him who I was, it wasn't hard for him to remember me, I was the young man who spoke 5 languages and was extremely honest during the home visit back on January 08, 2002. I told him that I called the INS and that I couldn't find the agent who was with him when my passport was taken. This FBI agent was a real gentleman with the full meaning of being professional and told me the following: "Yeah I can remember the INS agent had his last mission on the day we visited you, and then he asked, "Are you all right Ahmed?" are you taking care of yourself? So I replied with a yes, but I didn't dare to ask about my passport, I don't why? Maybe I didn't want to know in the first place, I am not sure. Before the agent hang up, he told me these exact words "Don't Worry". I thanked him and hung up with some peace of mind. That particular incident made me so eager to have the chance one day to work with the FBI or any other agency that serves the purpose of differentiating between good and bad.

My friend from the convenience store suggested me to move out of my apartment and live with him, since he was living by himself, and in that case, I could save up some money during the crises I have been going through. Without planning or thinking I agreed to the suggestion because it seemed right at the moment, and that's where we humans always tend to fall, simply by our own mistakes, what seems right for the moment turns out to be wrong in the long run; yet how would we know when we can't foresee the future!!

He was a nice friend, the truth has to be said and he always did cook for both of us, he was truly an amazing cook, but he had some attitude issues that I had to deal with, and since I was living under his roof, I had to go along with everything. I wasn't as free as I used to be. It was really hard. The more it got further complicated when my queen called me up crying from her friends whom she was living with, those friends were against her relationship with me for reasons I was never able to grasp, they treated her all of a sudden as a third-class citizen, trying to control her just because she was living with them. I couldn't accept a situation like this; in the first place, she came all the way from California to Texas to be with me. So, I had to request my friend to extend his courtesy and let me bring her into the apartment, just until I find a new place, I couldn't let her face such kind of treatment, no matter what the consequences would be. Thankfully, my friend agreed, and right the next day I went to pick up my queen from her place. She only had a couple of bags, so it didn't take us long to move out from her friends' house.

A new yet twisted and hard relationship started, we lived in together but weren't really alone, despite that we had our own room. As much as I was very thankful to my friend for his help, but his comments at times were just way too much, I think this was his way of life, he was simply himself. A few days passed and everything was all right until my friend needed help, this help involved my time, my car, and money as well. He was trying to open a convenience store in Waco City which required me to drive 200 miles back and forth just to help out. I couldn't refuse because it was a simple payback for his extended help.

But the pressure was rising, since I also had to drive my girlfriend to her work and pick her up as well wherein, she was working as a Nurse in a clinic. I really tried my best to please her and be totally supportive despite my hanging situation.

One day she woke up on the wrong side of the bed and opened up the subject of religion again, it really pissed me off because I felt that it was her style to create a fight out of nothing. My love for this girl, however, was just so extreme that I swallowed up all her crap, but it wasn't easy at all. Later that day I found out why she was so cranky, she needed a Thousand Dollars to pay for school in order to change her status from visitor to student, otherwise, she had to fly back to the Philippines. I was and I am still wondering why when problems and hardship fall on someone's head; they simply have to come all together! Why isn't that the case with happiness and joy? Nevertheless, I borrowed the amount for her and helped her out, I wanted to be the man she could count on, and I wanted to prove to her that despite of any and all obstacles we could make it. Life however had to always spice things up for me, to the extent that it was too damn spicy already. I left my job at the convenience store because the workload was too high, and the efforts exerted were not appreciated, and on top of that, the owner didn't even want to increase the wage. I had to find a replacement job as soon as possible since without work I wouldn't be able to survive.

Indeed, with my experience in running gas stations and convenience stores, it didn't take me long to find a job, but everything came with a price, despite that the owners were very nice or so they appeared at first, but they turned out to be very distrustful, after almost 3 Month's working with them they accused me with stealing from their cash register. That hurt me tremendously because I am the type of person who would rather die than commit something like that. Of course, I am surely not a saint; I made many mistakes in my life, but stealing was never one of them. The sad part was that they never even investigated it; they just threw that accusation at me. At that time I had an Iranian friend who was away for quite some time, and I had his credit cards with me, I am sure my mistake was when I used my friends' cards, several times even, but no one knew that I was paying his bills while he was away. The owners never even gave me the chance to explain anything, they just accused. I lost my job because of an employee who rubbed them, and I even knew who it was, but it wasn't my place to tell. The owners wanted to play smart and accused with something terrible that I didn't and wouldn't ever do. I guess this is just life, whenever you are too honest and too caring you just get stepped on. At least that's how it was in my case. Things didn't stop at that, my dear friend whom I was living with also turned on me after he decided to move and live in Waco city and requested me to take care of the apartment where we were at. I refused politely and explained to him that I will be moving as well since I had no longer a job in Dallas and I didn't want to stay there anymore after what had happened, besides that, I wanted to be in an area which was closer to my girlfriends' workplace. My dear friend didn't like it and moved out the next day and left me a note that said "Don't forget who you are, what you are and where you came from" I didn't even understand what his problem was and why he left me an insulting note like that? I did more than anyone would do for him to show my gratitude, yet it seemed that it was never enough for him.

A few days later, I and my girlfriend started to look for a new place that was not too far from her clinic and we found an amazing place in Frisco City. We moved out of Dallas and began our new journey in Frisco. It was a rough start because I was jobless, and I started to use up my simple savings. The pressure on me was just too high, and the fear of the unknown was hunting me continuously.

After some time another religion argument came up, yet out of love; I told her that I am willing to go with her to the biggest most known Catholic Church of her choice and that I was willing to meet up with the high priest of the Church to discuss our case, and at the same time for me to ask the Priest a few questions related to religion. I told her that if the Priest answers my questions in a straight way that is logic and convincing then I'll convert, but if not, then she can stay on the belief she's holding and so should be the case with me. And indeed that's what happened, we scheduled a date and went to Church, the Priest was a very nice man and very accommodating, and after he heard our story, he mentioned that religion is a choice and not a demand, so it's up to us to respect each other's perspective way of beliefs or not, which basically reflected what I was telling her all along. Then I asked the priest my questions, but he didn't really answer them, he just gave the philosophy and the ideas about the topics; But never an answer.

After the meeting we thanked the priest for his precious time and left, my girlfriend was silent and it actually worried me, because her silence was never a good indicator. Nevertheless, I felt that I did everything for the sake of this relationship and just hoped for the crises to fade away. Some time passed without having this topic opened; until one day we went out to eat something at Cheesecake Factory; it was a black day for me because my girlfriend surprised me with her complete determination of having our relationship ended due to religion again. A topic that popped out of the blue and without prior notice; a topic which I tried to avoid as much as possible and only discussed with her when she was on top of wanting to argue. I didn't only get pissed, but was mad as hell, and asked her why she didn't tell me that prior to making our big move to Frisco? Why did we move then together in the first place? Why did we even bother to go to church and seek for consultation then?

After the bitter fight we left the restaurant and went back to our apartment, I didn't know what to do and I didn't know why my life had to be like this? We didn't talk to each other from the moment we stepped into the apartment and at night I slept alone in the living room. The whole night my thoughts were wandering, and I just wanted to have a final solution to this drama. The next morning the strangest thing happened, instead of packing my bags and leave and instead of talking about what had happened; I proposed to her, I asked for her hand despite the huge fight we had the day before. The weirder it got, she agreed and without any arguments even. I guess that each one of us was just simply crazier than the other.

Within a week time everything was arranged, and we got a date in court, we bought the rings, her dress and my suit and even informed our families on the phone. A friend of hers came from Chicago to join our special day and so was the case with me, wherein, one of my friends in Dallas came with his wife. And so it was, on January 31, 2003 we were officially husband and wife.

A big step in my life where I had totally no clue what I got myself into, when you love you are basically blinded, and you only wish and anticipate the best outcomes. Well, my case had to be very special as usual, simply because I had to face many hard and complicated issues at the same time. Just a few days after my marriage I had to consult with an attorney because the situation in the USA was heating up due to two things:

> The first was the announcement of the Department of Immigration who demanded "Nonresident Arab Applicants" to file for fingerprints and "Special Registration".

> And the second was the implementation of a new department called "Homeland Security" which was to be active on March 01, 2003

My fear was tremendous, because my passport wasn't with me in the first place, and I didn't even know where it was, I was supposed to have a court hearing which was never scheduled, my case was lost in the system and the INS officer who interviewed me was already retired. And on top of that I was Jobless and newly married. It seemed to me as if I won the Jackpot.

The attorney advised me to be out of the USA before March 01, 2003, but I had two main obstacles, my passport and my new wife.

So my attorney requested me to purchase a plane ticket to any destination of my choice without worrying about the issue of my passport. Then she explained to me that this move is considered a showing of good faith and that it had to be done the very soonest possible. Of course I listened to her advice and I did what she requested. Two days later I went back to my attorneys' office with a return ticket to Jordan dated the 28th of February 2003, I had to choose Jordan since that was the only destination open and available for me.

My attorney was indeed very professional and very helpful; I put my entire trust in her which she totally deserved. The meeting on that day didn't last long; all she did was to take a copy of my ticket and told me to wait for her phone call.

The days were moving very slowly, the sadness of my wife killed me, and the anxiety of waiting ate me up, but of course I had no choice. Though the positive side of all that was that I had a break from the religion issues with my wife; all we talked about was what will happen next and what was there to be done?

As much as I wanted her to be with me in going back to Jordan, but it seemed impossible at that point, she had to work, and she had to pass her "Nursing Board Exam" which was the only gate for her to become a legal resident of the USA.

A few days later my attorney called, and she asked me to urgently give her a visit. And without even hesitating I jumped into my car and drove right the moment. This was the fastest time I ever reached the office of my attorney.

As soon as I entered her office, she handed me my passport, I was totally speechless and quite frankly I didn't even grasp it, how? How did this happen? What was the story behind? Thankfully my attorney didn't let me wait for long and told me that I had a high recommendation from the FBI and that's why my passport was kept, giving me the chance to stay in the USA until I could change my status. Sadly, that change of status never happened and was almost impossible in a case like mine. Then she added and informed me that since my passport is with me now, my leaving is considered a voluntary departure and not a deportation, yet as per law I should be escorted by a deportation officer, nevertheless, I was given a further chance to prove my good intensions and my sincerity. Then she gave me the phone number of the deportation officer who should have been responsible for me in case a voluntary departure didn't happen. My attorney advised me to call her and arrange with her what I should do to prove my departure after it occurs. I had a total overload of information and nothing was actually easy. Then lastly, she advised me to depart from Houston Airport and not from Dallas, I didn't quite get it why? But I just followed her instructions to the letter.

As soon as I stepped out of my attorney's office I called the deportation officer's number, introduced myself and explained to her what I was told by my attorney, then she replied with "Oh yeah, I know all about you" and then she added "stick to your word and just leave on the given date, don't let me regret giving you this chance" I of course assured her that I would not beat around the bush and that I will do what is required from me. I thanked her for the trust she gave me, then she said "you are the first person ever in my career who thanked me for letting him/her leave, it seems that what I heard about you is true" and then she added "when you arrive your destination, just send me a copy of your boarding pass and a copy of your entry stamp, so that I can register it in the system in order for you to be on the safe side for future purposes"

Once again, I assured her that I will do everything that is required of me, thanked her one more time and we hung up. At that moment, despite of the added pressure of having to leave my wife behind and the fear of what might happen at the airport, I was kind of relieved that I knew already what was going on, and that my passport was between my hands already.

Just a few days left till my departure date, I was furious, nervous and most importantly sad, not only I was leaving my wife behind, but the country itself; I haven't felt such a strong attachment and belongingness to any country I've been to, other than Germany of course and Israel.

These days, the warm connection between me and my wife escalated, she became more romantic and more sensitive, and that's when we started to call each other "Honeybunch".

I know that everything in life happens for a reason, but the problem is that we are only humans; we are not always capable of understanding, and to keep accepting everything the way they are, is just too damn hard. And so, that was basically my case, totally torn apart, yet I had to make use of the few remaining days I had left in the USA, so I tried to spend the best time possible with my "Honeybunch".

The closer the day for leaving approached the heavier my chest got and the pretending of having a fabulous time wasn't just effective anymore.

And like a blink of an eye dooms day was in front of my doorstep, February 28, 2003. I, my wife and my friend who attended my simple wedding drove to Houston Airport. With tears and endless hugs we said our goodbyes.

After bags inspection I stood in a long line of passengers, but then there were officials going through, checking on passports, when my turn came, I was taken out of the line and asked to follow them, honestly, I felt as if my heart was slipping down my feet. Apparently, it had to do with the region my passport was issued from. Nevertheless I was at a smaller line and the inspection was done quickly despite the escalated security issues. At the airlines counter it also went smooth, and I was finally done with the whole pressure, fear and anxiety, all I had to do was to wait for my plane to depart. While I was waiting my tears just couldn't stop from falling, no matter how hard I tried. I simply just didn't want to return but sadly had no choice at all.

It was a long flight back to Jordan, but I reached the destination. When I submitted my passport at the passport counter the policeman asked me to step aside and gave my passport to some other guy, then I was taken into an investigation office that belonged to the Jordanian FBI. Of course I was kept waiting before anyone talked to me, and it took almost an hour. Everybody who was on my plane left the airport and my family was still waiting for me, not knowing what was going on. When the officer started questioning me, he actually wanted to know how I left the USA without having any troubles; it was so strange for me and nothing really made sense. Eventually I pulled out my "American Marriage Certificate" and told him that I came back to Jordan to process my papers and that it wasn't possible for me to stay in the USA at this time. The Agent then didn't push it any further and wished me the best of luck. Finally this nightmare was over, and I got to see my family who patiently waited for me.

As much as I was happy to see my family as much I was in pain and sadness, yet I knew I had to be strong enough to keep going. When I reached my dad's house, I called up my wife to let her know that I arrived safely and that everything went fine despite of the events that I had go through. She was so happy when I called her because the stress that she had to go through was also so tremendous.

Later that evening I saw my kids and it truly felt great, but at the same time I felt the distance and the gap. Of course I knew that their mother was poisoning them with words of hatred, and there was nothing I could do at that stage. I tried to deal with it by being who I am; I dealt with them by reflecting love and made them feel it. The task was hard, but what was easy in my life anyway?

Right the next day of my arrival I went to the post office and send an express mail to the officer in the USA as I have promised her. My boarding pass, a copy of my passport and a copy of the entry stamp to Jordan. I fulfilled my obligation.

My daily life was really dull, but I tried my best to look at the bright side which I actually couldn't see. So I kept doing the best I could, towards my family, my kids and of course my wife who I left behind in the USA.

A new cycle of life started, and I learned something new: "Long Distance Relationship", this is surely not something that I would recommend to anyone, but sometimes circumstances are simply stronger than us, and in that case we don't stand a chance but to go through it.

My wife kept calling me almost every day, just to narrow down the physical distance between us and make life in a way possible. This situation kept going that way, until early May 2003, a day when my wife told me that she was two months pregnant and that she would want to be with me rather than being alone in the USA. She told me that she would do her NCLEX exam at a later stage. Of course this news made me very happy but at the same time fearful of her reaction being in the Middle East for the first time, since not all people can adopt a new way of life.

I took the matter very seriously and started to look for a nice and specious apartment to make her feel all right. I bought new furniture and prepared as much as I could.

Eventually the plan pushed through and my wife arrived in Jordan, she was so very welcomed by my family wherein, they made her feel as if she was part of the family since ages. The first few days were actually Ok, despite that she wasn't used to the kind of food with spices we had, but since we were at my parent's house still; she was able to mingle with the people of the house despite the language gap. Once we moved to the apartment which I had prepared for her, she literally started having a culture shock, just as I anticipated. I tried my best to comfort her and do whatever was in my power to make her feel good. Sometimes it worked and sometimes it didn't. She was going through a lot at that time, everything made her angry and restless, out of the simplest things there were arguments, yet I took it all in, because I wanted her to feel home. The situation wasn't easy at all for me, most especially that I was going through a symptom called "Couvade Syndrome" that is a situation when a man is from head to heels in love and goes through the entire pregnancy symptoms, and in my case it wasn't a sympathetic stage, I in fact felt everything for her and instead of her, I am the one who had the morning sickness and the vomiting and I am also the one who had the cravings. It was just simply crazy, and on top of that I had to deal with her mood swings and culture shock issues. Yet all of that I considered as being normal, and I convinced myself that we had to go through this transformation period one way or the other. But what happened next, was just not among the normal anymore. A day before her birthday we went to my family and stayed there, it was supposed to be a surprise for her, wherein my family wanted her to feel great and not being deprived of anything, and actually were preparing cakes, food and a simple yet nice birthday environment. Yet, at night my wife was in a really bad mood, so bad that she was totally insane, it was just about 30 minutes before midnight. She didn't wait to be surprised and instead she was the one to surprise me with her insanity and told me "I want to go back to the Philippines" at first, I didn't grasp it, but she was so serious that I couldn't have missed it. So, I wanted to discuss this with her as it is supposed to be done between any couples when any issue arises. But she was just so snob about it and told me "This is my final decision" so I got really mad because this is not an individual issue, this was a family issue we were talking about, and so I asked her "And what about our son? You are still pregnant" she answered me "and so? I am taking my son with me" that really made me flare up and I started yelling "what do you mean? You will not even let me see my own son? Do you really have a heart for such? She answered me back with complete rudeness and sarcasm, as if I was dealing with some other woman and not my own beloved wife. At that very minute she told me that it was her final decision and made me appear as if I had no existence; I truly have no idea how I reached to the height of my emotions and all my anger came out with one slap on her face, but I felt so terrible doing it, because I always believed that hitting a woman is definitely not manhood. I started hitting my own hand against the wall to punish myself for slapping my wife. Despite all the previous troubles that I had to face in life, I never encountered such, so it was new to me and I just didn't know how to react towards losing my son who wasn't even born yet; and on top of that, for no valid reasons. Of course my entire family barged into the room when they heard the noise, this family who was actually preparing to surprise my wife with a nice simple birthday party, yet instead they are the ones who got surprised with our fight together. So they took me out of the room and stayed with her. My family stood with her wholeheartedly and tried their best to comfort her. They were telling me that she has no one here in Jordan and that the feeling of being a stranger in a new country can affect anyone. They were coming up with all different alibis for her and she was just so snob.

I took a deep breath and tried to cool down, I felt sorrier for her than I felt sorry for myself, but I was internally destroyed and scared. So I requested my family to leave the room so that I could talk it over again with my wife. Now this time she was just listening and didn't say a word. I told her that I was truly sorry for using my hand and that it will never ever be repeated again, I also told her that she was pushing me beyond the threshold of any human being. Yet, I shouldn't have slapped her.

Then I told her that my family and I were preparing a surprise party for her, but instead we all got surprised with what had happened. I also explained to her that she can think it over all night long wherein, I will not be with her in the room so that she can have her space and time alone, I also assured her that if she really wanted to go to the Philippines that I am totally ready to go as well, for as long as we are not going to destroy our own family. It's not only us; there is an innocent baby involved who didn't even see the sunlight yet.

I wasn't able to sleep the whole night; it was just a nightmare for me, for one, being mad and upset on the unexpected turn of events, the guilt of having slapped my wife, even if it was just once, and the fear of what's yet to come. I also was thinking about the travel to the Philippines when there's no alternative left.

As early as 7 in the morning I went to my wife to check on her, she was awake, in fact she didn't sleep at all just like me. I apologized to her once again and asked her to forgive me for this one incident, wherein, I shouldn't be blamed for my reaction. I explained to her that my feeling at that very moment was as if someone was taking my soul out of my body. She actually understood my point and really felt bad, she even stated the following words "Your slap made me wake up and I am sorry for how I behaved" she cried afterwards, and we embraced each other. I felt so sorry for her and I just wanted to do anything even if it was beyond my power and capacity.

So, I thought in order to have this issue resolved and make my wife happy even if it was just a temporary solution, I should make a move, and so I decided to travel to the Philippines with my wife; for one to get to know her family, just the way she got to know mine, and for her to be home for a few days which would lessen the pressure on her with the fast moving events we had to face during a short period of time; and on the other hand to meet up with a company in Manila for the purpose of a certain business. At the time I got married and was still in the USA. My wife and I received a simple wedding gift from one of her sisters in the Philippines; this gift was a pendant that had our pictures engraved on it. I liked the idea so much and thought this might be a nice business to engage myself with in Jordan.

However the problem was that I didn't have enough money in hand especially after all the expenses I had to face in opening a new home prior to my wife's arrival. So I introduced the project to a friend of mine to be my partner. It actually didn't take long for him to agree, because he was so convinced with the business and was looking forward to it already. With this turn of events the multipurpose trip to the Philippines pushed through and on the first week of June 2003 we left for the target destination.

And so it was, we arrived the Philippines and even were picked up by my wife's elder sister and her husband; I had a good first impression, but it's definitely not always a good sign. We were driven to their small tight simple house in a place called "Malate" The weather was hot and humid, and the language spoken was surely new to me. Yet, I didn't bother myself with it; I knew that it's just a short stay and my goal was to get to know my wife's family and to make the best out of the business that I intended to engage myself in.

So my first Asian tour and experience started from that point, this place was simply different, crowded, hot and something strange was bugging me, but it was too early for me to find out what it was, it was too early for me to understand.

We stayed the whole first week in Manila, which gave me enough time to meet up with the company several times and get trained using the engraving machine, I also had ample of time to make my pendants purchases.

During this week the elder sister of my wife was throwing words at me, but made it appear as if it was a joke, she was stating "why don't you divorce my sister, and I will pay you" and then continues to laugh. At first, I didn't want to think negative, and I was just returning an answer in the same style and manner, laughing and answering, "it will not happen, even if you pay the world to me". As much as I was bothered from the inside, but I just wanted to give the benefit of the doubt and tried to stay cool, calm and not to make an issue out of something that might turn out to be just a joke for real. But what a bad joke indeed if it was one!!

After that, we left the house of the elder sister and took a plane to the city where the rest of my wife's family lived, a city called "Cagayan De Oro" which was about an hour and 20 minutes flight away.

The city appeared to be nice, small and cozy and so much less stressful than the capital city. The thought alone of being away from a nagging old witch was indeed a relief. So here it was, I met with my in-laws for the very first time. At the airport I met 1 brother, 2 sisters and whole bunch of her nieces and nephews. On the way to their house they stopped at the cemetery for my wife to visit her passed away dad, they had a prayer there, stayed for a while and had a chit chat. For me, I was just basically observing and trying to understand the nature of the people. There wasn't much really going on with me, it was only one of her sisters who was talking to me, since she really had good English skills, but with the rest, they were describing their English with "Nosebleed". After almost 40 minutes at the cemetery we continued our way heading towards my wife's house or rather her family's house. There I met my so called "mother in law" and the remaining members of her family. But honestly, I wasn't impressed at all with how my wife's mother greeted us, and I realized from that moment that things won't be easy at all, yet and again I didn't want to jump into conclusions. What was bothering me the most was that they all were speaking their language including my wife; and of course I had to wait for a translation to be made; a situation that makes you feel as if you are a total outsider or an intruder, what is even more bothersome is when you realize that these people actually know enough English to communicate yet chose not to.

Well, I tried my best not to have my multipurpose journey to the Philippines be spoiled, and I tried constantly to be positive, I also did my best to give the benefit of the doubt and convinced myself that maybe things like these are just normal in their culture. But as the days passed, I've noticed and couldn't simply ignore the fact anymore, that it's all about two major things, one is MONEY and the second is RELIGION. We were basically going out on a daily basis, to eat shop and unwind, but most of the times my wife's brothers, sisters or nieces and nephews had to be part of it. Very seldom I was alone with my wife during that time.

Not to mention that the few times we ate at the house we basically participated with the expenses or even paid it all. It was totally surprising to me; most especially that we were supposed to be the guests. Yet here the trend was for the guest to shoulder everything!!! Every time we planned to window shop or just go for walk at the mall, someone had to be with us, and mostly we ended up paying for whatever was chosen by them. It was obvious already that my wife was trying to buy their love and made me part of it. I wasn't mad at the money we spent; I was internally mad about the way it was done. They literally considered us as milking cows. Nevertheless, I haven't showed my frustration but was talking it over with my wife when we had the chance, but she kept telling me "it's my family". Here a big question came to my mind, so what's the case if we didn't have that money to spend? What would've been the outcome? However, since I had no intensions at that time to actually be in the Philippines other than visiting, I let these questions just pass by without actually giving it any serious thoughts. Was that a mistake? Well, time will definitely tell.

A whole month passed by and all I could say was "wow" I spent US$5,000 during the 3 weeks we spent with my wife's family. Seriously, it wouldn't have been a problem or an issue if it wasn't just done the hustlers' way. In the end I did this whole thing for the sake of my wife and nobody else.

Being in love sometimes can be a curse, dreaming about the future and having a loving family is a challenge, most especially when you deal with a culture that you have no clue about.

And so our journey to the Philippines finally ended, especially for me; and we flew back to Jordan. This whole new experience was indeed tough, but again and for the sake of my love, for my wife, and my unborn son, I just took it all in and hoped for the best.

Of course with all the expenses shouldered in the Philippines and the cost for the engraving machine and pendants I reached rock bottom, so I had to make miracles happen to start the business the soonest possible, otherwise I would end up totally broke, and from experience, being a family man you can't allow yourself to be broke, otherwise it will hit you hard and harder than you can imagine.

My partner and friend who paid half of the expenses prior to my leaving to the Philippines was totally ready and excited for the business, since we were the first to open this kind of project in Jordan, our expectations were high, and we were very optimistic. He even surprised me that our store inside the mall was ready and he made it look so unique with the design he made; wherein, his main profession is interior designer; so I had a so called perfect partner.

We signed a contract with the mall owners, and we were officially operational in August, 2003. Where we opened was a new shopping mall, so we basically opened with the opening of the mall itself. Our business name was catchy; wherein, I used the nickname of my wife and added the word "Collection". We actually had a good start and people loved the idea that we presented. However, to every upside there is a downside, I spent many hours at work leaving my wife at home with no one around her to talk to, she was living in a huge apartment but basically alone. Despite that our rented apartment wasn't that far from the mall, I didn't have the chance to always go home during the day to check on her, but of course I was calling her constantly when I had the chance. I even asked her to come to the mall since she had nothing to do, but she was right, what will she do? She will get bored eventually, especially when I am busy and have no time to entertain her. Sometimes she came and spent a few hours and sometimes she just stayed the whole day at home. It was indeed a big challenge for the both of us, I had no choice but to work and she had nothing else to do. When this situation went on like this, in the second month problems started to arise, she was most of the time in a really bad mood, we were arguing almost all the time and we were even talking about divorce like almost every day. It was such a painful time. What triggered this situation even more, was that despite the business was doing well, most of the money earned was used for our daily needs, the mall's high rent, our apartment rent and the percentage for my partner, so basically what came in came out with no saving chances. So one night she was really on the height of her bad mood, she opened the fridge and started yelling "what's the need of having such a big high tech fridge when it's empty?" So I just stood there and answered "empty?" "It is nice to be thankful for what we have; the fridge might not be as full as you want it to be, but it's definitely not empty, what we have inside that fridge to some people it's already a lot" Instead of answering she immediately jumped to another topic and started yelling "why such a big apartment? What do we need it for?" so I realized it was just a way to make things difficult, and I didn't know how to please her? What will I answer her? No matter what I say I'll be at fault. But since it's my nature not to leave questions hanging I answered her "Is that now bad in your eyes that I wanted you to feel like a queen? I know that I don't have the capacity to make you live like a real queen, but I am trying with everything that I have and can, can't you even see that, can't you even sense that? What am I supposed to do to satisfy you when everything that I do is already an issue to you? Isn't it better to have a bigger place than having a small place? Can you predict the future? Why are you doing this?" She jumped into the triggering topic and started talking about religion, my God I was so exhausted from work and now I had to deal with an additional night shift of my wife's mood swings. It seemed that the fight and argument won't end, and so I just begged her to have a continuation of this episode the next day, because I simply knew that I won't get anywhere with this, she will keep jumping from one topic to another without making any progress.

I took a shower and slept with an empty stomach; how could I eat when she fed me with all her endless complaints? I really was lost again and didn't know what to do? But I was wondering what makes her likes this. Is it really because she has nothing to do? Or is it because she's alone? Or is it because she's pregnant? I was thinking of everything and all the possibilities, but I never thought that some of her so called friends and family members were feeding her with whatever ideas and poisonous thoughts. Apparently, there is something in the Philippines that is called "crab mentality", I didn't discover that at that time, but it became clear to me at a later stage of my life with her. This "crab mentality" focuses on destroying a person's will by dragging him or her down to the far bottom of hell. Filipinos use this against each other, and it's known by all of them, it doesn't matter if the person is your friend, a family member or just an acquaintance, they just simply use it whenever they feel like it. So in one way or the other it was used on her and she took the bait, despite that she knows all about the "crab mentality", but sometimes people make it appear as if they care for you and as if they advise you, but the reality is that they just want to make your life hell. What kind of sickness is that? I really have no clue? But that's just how it is.

The next day I didn't go to work and just stayed home to make things up, even though I didn't know what to make up? Since there was nothing that I can remember that I did wrong; but I opted to give it a shot, so I prepared breakfast and woke her up with a kiss. At first, she said she doesn't want to eat, but I insisted and told her that I am not going to work for that day. Finally she stood up, washed her face and came to the kitchen, and we ate but were very quiet, not a single word was spoken. After we finished eating, I stood up to clean up the table, but she didn't let me, that's the time she spoke and said "I'll be the one" so I didn't say a word because I was scared that maybe it will turn into another argument, I was having phobias already on how to deal with her. So in order for me to say something and open a conversation, I asked her if she needed anything from the supermarket since I wanted to buy some juice. She nodded her head, and my attempt was unsuccessful. So I excused myself and left the apartment to buy the juice, on my way I stopped at an internet café to check my emails, since I was out anyway and never had that much chance to check my emails while I was at work, but nothing worth mentioning was in my inbox. So, I checked online for an alternative place to buy blank engravable pendants from, since the company I dealt with in the Philippines was charging me pretty high prices. However, my mind was so totally with my wife, and not in what I was doing, I wanted to have the power to make her happy and feel at ease, I just didn't know how? So I left the net, went to buy the juice and then returned home. She was still in the kitchen just seated, so I told her "let's talk but please let's try not to have a fight." And the discussion went on, I told her "The way religion is important to you, it's also important to me; I do respect your way and as I told you from the start that Islam states clearly that every person has the full right to choose his own path, there's no such thing as forcing, otherwise it won't be a religion anymore. Our fights and arguments when we speak about religion are coming from your side and not mine; I even went with you to a priest in the USA to prove you, my side. So, why keep doing this? If you want to stay as Christian that's your choice and I respected it from the very start and will keep respecting it till the end, but when it comes to our kids, we have to find a solution to that, and a solution is not by fighting honey. She answered exactly these words "they will follow me" So with this kind of an open closed statement I knew it's useless to continue with a discussion, otherwise it will be a fight again and I just couldn't take it anymore.

Our life wasn't really easy, but I just tried my best and simply didn't give up. My love for this woman kept me going despite that it was a rough route, and I convinced myself that she also wouldn't be hanging in there if she wasn't having the same feelings or at least close to it.

I called my mom asking her for advice; I was somehow frustrated and scared; I didn't know how to deal with this situation anymore. So my mom asked me one simple question "do you pray Ahmed?" and my reply was "No, what has this to do with what I am asking you about?" she replied "It's simple my son, no matter how strong you think you are, no matter how smart you are, there are instances in life, just like this one, where you will get stuck and you need an upper power to help you, and in order to seek help you have to be close to HIM all the time and not only at times of needing help." Then she continued "how can you have a positive effect on any person in life when you yourself are not doing what you are talking about, son, you can't give what you don't have. Pray and ask guidance and help, you will feel and see the change".

Indeed I followed my mom's advice, but it wasn't easy because I felt so disconnected, so when I stood on the praying rag to pray, I wasn't able to read, I was just crying and crying. My wife saw me and for the first time having the attempt to pray, but it was strange, instead of seeing me pray I was just crying. I tried to focus, I tried to control myself, but my tears just wouldn't stop. So I sat on the floor with really red sore eyes and my hands covering my face. My wife approached me and was just an angel at that moment; she asked me "what's wrong?" so I told her that I was trying to pray but I just couldn't control myself, so she brought me a glass of water, kissed my cheek and told me to go wash my face and try again. After around 15 minutes I calmed down, washed my face and tried again, and yes, I was able to pray. From that day on, I kept praying even if at times I'd miss it, but I never stopped praying. So my wife kept seeing me even if I was praying in a different room.

A few days later she requested me to take her to a church, and since I always believed that every human being has the right to have his own faith, I wholeheartedly took her the next day. But it didn't help much, because the prayer was in both Arabic and Greek. So she stayed there for about 20 minutes and left. I was waiting for her outside and got surprised why she left so early, she thanked me for taking her and told me that she just wanted to be in the house of God, and besides that, she didn't really understand. Yet she was happy and felt like eating outside, and so we went to a shopping mall, had a late lunch and ate sweets at Cinnabon afterwards; probably one of our best days in Jordan up to that day. Time passed by and work was going well, but there was a close eye watching us, the owners of the mall were greedy bastards and wanted to take our business' concept, in fact they wanted our shop in particular.

So, that wasn't really a good sign and working became a pressure. Yet, I guess when you sometimes ignore, especially ignorant people; you are just basically doing the right thing, otherwise, everything and everybody will get on your nerves.

By the first week of October my wife was getting close to delivery or rather being in her month. There was excitement from my family and her, but on top of them all, it was me, I was waiting for the moment, I never had such a feeling before despite of having 3 children from my previous failed disaster; I won't call it marriage because I truly don't believe it was.

Anyway, we were constantly visiting my wife's Ob-Gyn during her pregnancy, but our visits became more often during this period. The relation between my wife and her Ob- Gyn was wonderful and exceeded the normal trend between Dr. and Patient. She was very attentive and close to my wife.

Then the awaited time finally came, delivery day was there. I took my wife to the hospital and even attended her delivery, and that is definitely not a normal trend in Jordan, but things you do when you are in love, you just go against any stream without even caring. While she was in the process of delivering she was holding my hand and suddenly she was in severe pain, she put her hand on top of mine and before I knew it, her finger nails were deep in my hand, it was so painful but I couldn't open my mouth cause my entire concentration was with her and her doctor, and of course I didn't want to sound as if I was also giving birth with her at the same time.

And here he was, Aladdin was born on the 28th of October 2003, a little tiny baby below average weight and with a clubfoot. When his mom woke up, she was so exhausted but asked for her son, he was brought to her and she had a huge smile on her face, then she said, "it was all worth it".

My whole family came to congratulate us. My mom stayed with us at our apartment for a whole week taking care of Aladdin and taking care of my wife who was really exhausted from giving birth.

The doctor informed us to make a daily massage on Aladdin's foot for it to be corrected. She also advised to have the same done for his nose, since he inherited a flat one from his mom. She explained that by giving a constant massage to the nose it will become better.

After my wife gave birth, she was so light, her aura was just so different, and she was so sweet. I really loved it but didn't mention anything; deep inside myself I was hoping it would remain like that. After my mom left, the responsibility of taking care of Aladdin was on both of us, and it wasn't easy at all, he was a fuzzy angry little boy, when he cried, he would cry so heavily that he would turn blue, to the extend we both would panic. These are unforgettable days indeed.

There was something big awaiting me which I had no clue about, not even the slightest hint. Something that I will always remember no matter what happens; on November 11, 2003 at 12.30 midnight my wife was restless in bed and even crying but silently, she didn't want to wake me up, wherein I slept early that day due to exhaustion from work and the lack of sleep from Aladdin who was waking up many times at night. Yet somehow, I felt her in my sleep and woke up. At first, I was thinking that I did something without noticing and really got worried, I just didn't want to be the cause of her tears. So I asked her what was wrong! But she just kept crying, so I went to the kitchen and brought her a glass of water. After she finished drinking, she asked me "can we talk?" wow, I literally felt my heart in my pants, I was sweating internally and was scared she would come up with another crazy idea, I had like a million thoughts crossing my mind that very second. Of course I would say yes to her, the topic must've been so serious for her to want to talk about it past midnight. So we left the bedroom and went to the kitchen for us not to wake up our baby.

I had no nerves left in me, I was so anxious but didn't want to show it to her, and I tried to control myself to the fullest.

Then I asked her "Is there anything I can do for you? Would you like to have a tea or something?" I was just trying not to show my fear from the unknown midnight topic. She replied, "No thank you, just sit down please." So I sat down and told her "I am all ears, please let me know what is bugging you, I just hope it wasn't me, because I truly can't remember saying or doing anything" she replied "relax, I just want to ask you something about religion" my heart at that moment was in race with time, I didn't want to have a midnight argument, most especially about a sensitive topic which always led to a dead end before. But I went along and told her "sure, what is it honey? I am always at your service."

Then here came the unexpected, she asked me what I never would've guessed, not even in a million years, especially from her.

She asked, "how does a person become a Muslim?" And I was like, huh? Seriously? Why? How come? What happened? What's wrong? All these were my facial expressions but not a single word came out of me. Then I asked her "what do you mean? Why would you be bothered with such a question and in the middle of the night? And why were you crying honey, what has this question to do with your crying? I am really puzzled here."

And she replied "Just answer me please and you will know" So I told her "It's simple, you just have to believe that God is ONE and that He has no partners, and that Prophet Mohamed is his last sent Prophet to humanity, and once you believe it, you state the following sentence in Arabic "Ashhadu an La Illaha Illa Allah, wa Ashhadu anna Mohamadan Rasul Allah" which means in English "I testify that there is no God but GOD alone, and that Mohamed is the Prophet of God" And that's it honey" at that moment she was just crying, and I started crying with her without knowing why? I was just having an open faucet of tears which came down without knowing why? I was simply crying because she was, and I wasn't able to control my tears anymore, they just kept flowing.

It continued like this for straight 15 minutes, no talk, just crying. Until she said "I know this sentence very well in Arabic, I just didn't know what it meant" so the more I was puzzled and asked "how? How do you know that, from where? And why now?" so she answered me "While I had nothing to do at home, I was reading the English version of the Quran for quite some time now, and I never told you about it, strangely, whenever I came by that sentence I found myself automatically repeating it over and over again without even knowing what it meant; until now when you explained that's how you become a Muslim after believing it."

I was just listening to her with an open jaw; I couldn't actually grasp it, simply because she used to literally give me Hell when a topic like this would be opened.

I accidentally looked at my watch and it was exactly 1.11 AM when she said, "I want to become a Muslim", not only Goosebumps I had, but my entire body was shivering. I don't know what was behind this date, but the date and time were extremely strange, and I think about it all the time. 11.11 At 1.11. If that was a coincidence! Then we are really living in a mysterious world where nothing makes sense anymore.

To make sure, I asked her "are you sure about this? Every person has the right to believe what he/she wants, don't change just to fit in" then she replied "No, I am just playing...OF COURSE I am sure, there are no games with issues like this."

After that she embraced me tightly and told me "forgive me for all the pain I have caused you" I was so speechless, all these events in one night unexpectedly, that was truly a blessing from God.

The next day, my family knew about what happened and came over to us including my children; they brought sweets and showed total support. My wife was never so happy, at least from the time I have known her.

Days passed by and everything was OK, except that winter started to set in, which meant less customers going to the mall which affected our business big time. The Mall owners took advantage of the situation and tried to take away our business in a sneaky way by having it made appear as if they were extending their help, they were saying, "how will you come up with the rent? The mall doesn't have many customers these days, why don't you just hand over your business and we will pay you for your work" So in other words they wanted me and my partner to become employees, not to mention that my partner worked 75% of the total mall's ceiling decoration with gypsum boards, the final pay amounting to $22,000 of his work wasn't paid to him to twist his arm and force him to accept. Yeah, it's a fact, there are many filthy and greedy bastards living on planet earth, and we just have to deal with it. But the decision we made was clear, we'd rather stop operating and even willing lose everything than giving it to a bunch of pricks.

And so we went on, survived the winter season and showed these greedy bastards that we were not an easy target. They on the other hand, sent us an official letter in March of 2004 that if we wanted to renew the contract that the rent will be increased 50%. So we knew right that moment that we were no longer to continue with this business at their mall, not even if they gave us the spot for free.

One morning I went to the internet café to make a pendants order and apparently it was time to have more spices on the chili time that I already had, a very strange email from an unknown person describing himself as a bank manager in Benin-Africa, the email was about a deceased customer who had 10.5 Million US Dollars deposited and had no next of kin, so his request was to have a legit transaction as per his explanation of presenting me as the next of kin since I carry the same last name, and that if it's not done that way, the money will just go in a wrong direction for people who don't even deserve it. He further explained in his email that the amount will be split between us once the transaction is complete. Well, honestly, I was overwhelmed and happy despite of being in doubt of the news, so I checked the name of the bank online and the phone numbers provided in his email to make sure of the accuracy of the information provided, it all appeared to be correct. This made me even more excited, and I emailed him back to send me an email explaining further about the legality issues. I left the internet café with high hopes and went back to my wife. Now I had some news to share with her, in the end 2 heads thinking is always better than one. She was surprised and couldn't believe it either, but it has given both of us some kind of hopes. At least my wife was kind of better off these days and wasn't in her constant bad mood anymore; that alone was surely a tremendous progress already.

The next day she prepared a nice breakfast, woke me up and told me to get ready to go to work, this gave me a good boost for the day and made me optimistic. Before heading to work I went to the internet café to check my mails again, excitement and nervousness were my partners at that moment, and here it was, an email from the man assuring me that it's an easy process with no need for me to go to his country and even requested for my phone number to call me at night and for us to keep in touch.

So I did, I wrote him back and provided my phone number as he requested yet I had the doubts that he will actually make an international phone call. After that I went to work and met up with my partner, it was my chance to seek another person's opinion that I trust and can depend on; so I told him about the email and my responses. He was surprised the same way I and my wife were surprised, at that time these stories weren't as rampant as it is in these days, even the overall usage of the internet wasn't as much. That's why falling for a story like this was likely possible.

After having discussed the topic, we came to the conclusion to wait and see where it will go, wherein we could simply back out at any time during the process if we had any doubts. At the end of the day my phone rang and without even checking the number I answered, and surprisingly it was the manager from the bank in Benin, he was indeed polite and very convincing on the phone, his call lasted for about 20 minutes explaining all the details of the procedure and the legality of it.

Of course I informed my wife about the progress of this topic, and despite of the thrill, there was this uncertainty dwelling within.

A few days later I received the news from the bank manager in Benin that the legal documents are ready, and a scanned copy was sent to my email, but in order for him to retrieve the original copies we had to pay him the amount of US$1,000. At first, I refused since the amount wasn't in hand in the first place, but the man had this amazing convincing power, in addition to that; the financial situation I was in, made me look at the big picture rather than at my current situation, it was like "what if?" My wife was present during the phone conversation and she commented with one word, "how?" so I knew she was in and willing despite of our financial difficulty. I called up my partner and explained to him what had happened, from his point of view it was risky but worth giving it a shot but, coming up with that amount at such short notice wasn't really easy. My wife opened one of the bedroom drawers and surprised me with some savings she had from the money that I was giving her from the business, she was trying to put some on the side for the rainy days, I also came up with some and the rest was paid by my partner, with that we had the total sum needed, and were able to send the money. There were 2 possibilities in front of us, either we will never hear from him again and that would mean it was a scam, or that the transaction is legit, and we might be lucky after all. Though the logic said that we were most likely to be victims of a Scam; so the only thing we were able to do was to simply wait and see.

Surprisingly, the man called and confirmed that he received the amount and stated that we need to be ready and that he's putting his faith in me, he further added and said "please don't become greedy and forget about our deal, my share is 50%" he also explained that the amount sent was to move forward with the transaction, since he can't use the amount that is in the bank, because it has not yet been officially released.

With this phone call of his, I, my wife and my partner were absolutely thrilled, and our hopes were sky high. The time after that was going tremendously slow, 3 days passed without hearing from him any word, until the 4th day at 7.30 AM, my phone rang, it was an international call, my sleepiness evaporated at that moment and I answered the phone with excitement; it really was him, until this very day I can't really describe my mixed emotions and feelings I had that moment, fear, excited, thrilled, nervous, happy, doubtful, all combined. He said the exact following words "keep an eye on your email today; you will receive an important mail from the Central Bank of Jordan, Goodbye".

Seriously, not even total mixed emotions are sufficient to describe that very moment, I started planning and thinking of all the things that I could do for my wife, family, kids, my beloved ones, and on top of all for the country itself. I left the house at around 9 AM, stayed at the internet café, opened my email and kept refreshing the page of my email, I was in a state of belief and disbelief at the same moment. I received several phone calls from my wife and my partner while I was refreshing my email page but there was still nothing, excitement and nervousness were simply tremendous to all of us; and suddenly here it was, an email sent from the Central Bank of Jordan, yet to be sure, I checked the spelling of the email address, letter by letter and compared it with the actual website of the central bank, and it was really 100% correct. The email's content was the following:

Attn: Mr. Ahmed Khalaf.

TRANSFER STOP ORDER BY THE FIU DEPARTMENT JORDAN

"Prior to the Central Bank of Jordan, regulation on foreign exchange transactions, under the issued anti-money laundering regulations designed to meet the FATF Forty Recommendations on Money Laundering, August 2001. Under Jordanian law, money laundering is considered an unlawful activity subject to criminal prosecution.

On October 8, 2001 revision to the Penal Code criminalized terrorist activities,specifically including financing of terrorist organizations. Be informed that Jordan ratified and became a full party to the International Convention for the Suppression of Financing of Terrorism on June 16, 2003. We as the central bank of Jordan has checked for assets of terrorists and terrorist groups identified by the United Nations 1267 Sanctions Committee. Be guided that prior to the early 2003 unconfirmed press reports that millions of dollars of charitable donations given to an unlicensed and unregistered Islamic charity in New York, were smuggled out of the U.S and subsequently laundered through our Jordanian banks in route to Iraq. There have also been investigations into the smuggling of cigarettes and other commodities into Iraq via a Jordanian network that laundered kickbacks to the regime of Saddam Hussein. The Central Bank of Jordan prior to the enacted a comprehensive anti-money laundering law, established under the established independent financial intelligence unit (FIU). Anti-money laundering codes of conduct as handled by the anti-corruption agency, with the Jordan Intelligence Services (JIS). Be informed that prior to the Jordanian officials report on financial institutions file of suspicious transactions reports and cooperation with prosecutors in line with the information related to narcotics trafficking and terrorism control. The Jordan Central Bank department of financial intelligence unit prior to the circular instructing financial institutions to be particularly careful when handling foreign currency/transfer acknowledgement transactions, especially if the amounts involved are large as yours or if the source of funds is in question as yours. Prior to the Banking Law of banking secrecy provisions in cases of suspected money laundering and terrorism financing. Note that prior to the Jordan 1988 UN Drug Convention ,the UN Convention against Transnational Organized Crime and the UN International Convention for the Suppression of the Financing of Terrorism conducts and in protocol to the Jordan Central Bank steps in constructing an anti-money and antiterrorist finance program, Specific anti-money laundering legislation recognizing all types of predicate offenses and in code of conduct to the Financial Intelligence Unit (FIU) that receives, analyzes and disseminates suspicious transaction reports to law enforcement agencies be informed that the Jordanian law Financial Crime Enforcement Network and Financial Intelligence Unit (FIU) of the Central Bank of Jordan hereby wish to inform you the funds and transfer received from Eco Bank Benin in the value of

USD$10,500,000.00 is hereby seized and blocked and you are hereby urgently requested to fax to this Bank via our Bank Fax Financial Crime Enforcement Network Drug/ Anti-terrorist Clearance secured in your name/funds from the country of origin of the transfer within 12 hours from now or else, the funds will be recalled seized as government of Jordan funds, blocked or recalled back to sender. Note that this funds in question has been booked/registered as Terrorist/Drug funds as the funds was illegally cleared from the sending bank, Eco Bank of Benin. Fax us the copy while you are required to bring the original in person and report to the the Jordanian law Financial Crime Enforcement Network and Financial Intelligence Unit (FIU) of the Central Bank of Jordan within 12 hours.

Note and be warned that there is NO ANY negotiation to this correspondence as any negotiation from you or any party related to you or this file other than the requirements herein will amount to total negligence of the law of Jordan and this will amount to the final seizure of the dirty Funds by the Jordanian law Financial Crime Enforcement Network and Financial Intelligence Unit (FIU).Be warned and follow accordingly for due cordial respect of the parties and banks concerned in this dirty/illegal transfer."

Now imagine yourself reading through such an email!!! How will you feel? How will you react? What will you think? A thousand questions will go through your head in seconds. My heart beats could not be counted anymore, and I was in a state that is simply indescribable. What the heck was that? Those were really big words and about things I had no clue about, nor did I want to have any clue about. Yet, I was at a point that we could call "No Retreat No Surrender". So I called up the phone number of the department which was included in the email. The secretary answered the phone; after I introduced myself, I went straight to the point and asked about the harsh email received. She asked me, wondering, when the email was sent. So I replied that it was just about 15 minutes ago. But she was positively sure that no email was sent on this day, at least not yet. She also assured that the emails from this department are being sent by her personally. Now my head was spinning, and I was just lost. She asked me to dictate the email address from where I got the email from, and when I did, she confirmed it was accurate. Then she asked me what the content was all about, and I explained to her that it was a transfer of funds amounting to 10.5M US Dollars. So, she asked me to wait and put me on hold, after about 5 minutes she was on the line again and told me that there is nothing in the system showing transfers of that amount. What else could I 've said aside from thank you? This was a total puzzle; I called up my partner and my wife and informed them about my conversation with the Central Bank; as for my wife she had a big loud sigh coming out of her and as to my partner, he simply couldn't be translated. Just minutes after my phone rang and guess who it was? The bank manager in Benin, he was shouting and yelling and told me "your people wanted to have the funds for themselves, so I pulled back the funds" then he hung up. Until this very day I am still not capable of grasping what had really happened? If it was a scam, then why would the guy call up several times after receiving what he was aiming for? To a person who performs a scam, the mission is considered accomplished as soon as the desired amount of money reaches to him or her, there is no need to actually follow up. So what was the case here? I never found an answer and never heard from the guy again, this incident remains a mystery. I learned a lesson though; people in general can't be simply trusted, most especially when you never even met them. In addition to that, when you are in a difficult financial situation you tend to believe whatever, you hear, it's like your inner self makes you want to believe what you hear, you want it to be true, and that's how you get dragged into a deeper hole. You start spending more money in projects and ideas that you have no clue about, in hope to get you out of your miserable situation, yet the outcome is just the total opposite. But when I think about the lessons learned by spending this USD 1000, it's kind of a good deal. So rather than taking it on a fully negative side, I opted to look at the positive side of it. That doesn't mean I didn't feel bad about it, but the bottom line is "lesson learned, and life goes on."

Of course as usual, life always had to surprise me with new things and here was just another one, my wife came up with the idea to try her luck in the USA one more time to pass her NCLEX exam for nurses, and from that point on to make our dream come true to eventually migrate. At that time Aladdin was only 6 months old, yet because I wanted to be a life partner who's fully supportive, I didn't object, in fact I did everything that was in my power to help out with the expenses of her travel to the USA. That's how it started of me being a father and a mother at the same time, it was tougher than you could imagine, but luckily, I wasn't totally alone, I had my family around me who could help me out, especially my mom. Being at work, dealing with the mall owners, taking care of my baby and dealing with my emotions of missing my wife; all of these combined was just more than too much.

My wife's plan was to work and study at the same time, so in order to save as much money as possible she stayed with some relatives in the US. It wasn't easy for her to be away from Aladdin, but she managed. In the end it was all for the sake of having a better future and in a place where we could be together with no financial issues to hunt us. We were communicating through emails and sometimes I had the chance to call her by phone.

As time passed by, the situation was getting harder, wherein it was just too hard for her finding a job while being illegal to work. So, she focused on studying and really studied very hard for the exam. Sadly, even with that she didn't have the luck; she didn't make it to pass the exam. Six months passed by, with no progress, so she decided to come back to Jordan. At that time I was living with my mom since I gave up the apartment which I rented, it made no sense for me staying in big apartment paying a high rent while being basically alone.

On the day of my wife's arrival, my family, me, and of course Aladdin were waiting for her at the airport. When she came, she seemed to be so happy being back, but she got hurt when Aladdin didn't accept her, he actually didn't know her. Of course Aladdin couldn't be blamed; he was just a One year old baby whose mother left him when he was barely 6 months old.

That time we were going through a rough financial period, for one my business was closed already after the contract expired in August of 2004 and was not renewed due to the greedy mall owners, and my wife's 6 months stay in the USA which was not a productive period; added to the declining of our financial situation. Nevertheless, we managed through, until my wife got really sick, she was diagnosed with hyperthyroidism and she needed an immediate operation, that's when I got stuck and didn't know what to do anymore, No one was financially capable to let me borrow, so my wife called up her family to ask for help, but the response was literally disgusting, they told her to come back to the Philippines and alone to have the operation made there, as to their say, it would be cheaper. All that was understandable and acceptable, but the emphasis of being alone was simply not right. When I knew this reaction, I vowed that even if I have to enslave myself, I will not let it happen for my wife to be humiliated directly or indirectly in anyway and by anyone, most especially by her family. So I started looking and searching for means until I came across the phone number of an ex-senator in Jordan. I called him up and explained to him my situation in details, indeed he was an Angel sent from heaven, despite that he didn't know me, he extended his help by directing us to a doctor's clinic for nuclear medicine, he told me to present myself and my wife as his friends and explained to me that he will cover the entire expenses for the operation. On the same day of this phone call we went to the clinic and there they scheduled my wife for the next day to have the operation done via nuclear medicine and not surgery. We were further informed that she could not be pregnant, nor can she be around anyone for the duration of a week after she gets treated via a dose of nuclear medicine and to have a place prepared for her in order not to affect anyone.

So, the next day was the day, she took the dose, and the treatment was done, however, the downside to this treatment is that she has to take medicine for life to get the needed hormones and have a balance of it, since the gland responsible for it has been burned by the intake if the nuclear medicine.

I had to arrange for my family to be away, so that she can be alone and not affect anyone with the radiation of the treatment she was given. Though in my case, I had to go to her to bring her food and whatever she needed, I didn't really care about getting affected, she was simply so much more important to me and her wellbeing was all I cared about. A whole week passed by, and everything was all right, but surprises had to be always present, in my case a surprise was always a new trial, and the weird part is that I barely stand up and barely catch my breath when a new strike comes in. Not much time passed after her operation until we found out that she was pregnant which was not evident nor known before she took the nuclear treatment. As we were advised, she should not be pregnant for 6 months after the intake of the nuclear medicine, simply because it can cause abnormalities to the fetus. At that point we didn't know how to react? My wife was kind of scared and was thinking of ways on how to check on the baby at early stages, for me I was ready to support her with whatever she decided, my family on the other hand, had the opinion of not giving up and to simply wait and see what miracles could do.

With this new turn of events my wife asked me about the possibility of trying to move out from Jordan and go to the Philippines, now since I didn't have my business anymore and since there was no income to support my growing family, I didn't want to stay in Jordan either, most especially that the country is really expensive, and I couldn't be depending on my family to keep supporting me and my wife and of course Aladdin. Furthermore, I also had the responsibility of my 3 other lovely children from my so called first marriage. So, I had to make a bold move and make sure that I have some funds left behind for my kids in Jordan and of course some funds to support ourselves in the Philippines, most especially that I already had a clear picture and full background on how important money is to her family. My only asset in hand was the engraving machine and the pendants left from the business which I closed, however, that asset wasn't only mine but my partner's as well, so I asked his permission to try selling the machine and the concept of the business since I will no longer be Jordan. He was hesitant at first, but when I explained to him the situation, he was really supportive and even told me that I can have the entire amount and not to worry about him. That of course was a relief and an unexpected help. Now my task was to find people who are interested in venturing into a new business and had the funds to pay the amount in cash. Luckily, it took me only 2 weeks to convince a business owner with the concept of my business, and the profit it could make, if the rent is not too high. Since he was already renting in one of the best malls in Amman at that time, he considered this as an additional profit, since he was paying the rent anyway. Yet the selling of the business wasn't that easy, there was a give and take regarding the price, eventually I was able to get around $7,000 for everything I had in hand. My wife also tried her luck to get some support from her family regarding the plane tickets, and they agreed to pay for her airfare however under the condition that it had to be paid back, it wasn't a shocker to me anymore since I knew that her family simply worships money, and everything is counted. I went along with it, so that we would not have to spend so much upfront losing all the money I had in hand, since we didn't know what was awaiting us there, yet we both wanted to be optimistic still.

The day of our departure arrived, and my family was so sad to see us leaving, most especially that they got so attached to Aladdin. But the circumstances called for it and it seemed that we had no other choices at that time. After a heartbreaking goodbye we went on our Journey to the Philippines, this time 3 people rather than only two. Safely we arrived in Manila and just like the last time, we were picked up by her elder sister and her husband including 2 of their kids. They were excited to meet our son, so basically Aladdin was our passport of being welcomed, if I could use that word, since I am writing it without even believing it.

We stayed for a few days in Manila since my wife's elder sister wanted to spend more time with Aladdin, and my wife made some medical follow ups and consultations regarding the operation in Jordan and also the unexpected pregnancy.

After that we flew to Cagayan De Oro, the city where the rest of the family was staying, and just like last time, a whole bunch of people were waiting as if they were happy. The same routine as last time, a stopover at the cemetery, eating and drinking, chit chat and playing and then driven to the house. Here we met my wife's mother again; we greeted her as it is supposed to be, and Aladdin was simply overwhelmed with all the new faces he encountered in the past few days, and he really didn't like his grandmother not even a single bit.

I didn't feel welcomed, and it bothered me, but I knew that I am doing this for the sake of my wife and son. The first few days were still alright, but HELL broke loose when my wife one night took the blood pressure of my so called mother in law and was asked why she didn't attend mass, so, she replied to her that she converted to Islam and that she wanted to tell her all a long but she didn't know how, she also told her that her brothers and sisters knew already and that she requested them not say anything until she gets the chance to talk to her personally and face to face. But none of my wife's words registered in the head of her mother, she totally shut down and became meaner than her usual attitude. My wife tried her best talking it out in a civilized way, but how could you be civil with people who only see themselves as right? Her mother told her in a firm and demanding voice that she needs to go to church the next day, but my wife refused and told her that it's her life now, and she added that religion doesn't come with force, it's simply a matter of faith. Nevertheless, my wife was hurt deeply, and she cried as if there was no tomorrow. I so much pitied her and was trying to comfort her as much as I could, but she was just so deeply hurt with all the words thrown at her. She was crying at my shoulder in our room that we were given, she was complaining about all the mistreatment she always received, she was telling me that she was never appreciated and that she was always the least in the family no matter what she did for them. These words came out of her mouth for the very first time; I never knew the situation was like that, before that moment. I was in a state of shock hearing my wife's words and the deep pain she was in; I couldn't believe that she had so much inside her and never told me a word about it. No wonder I had these strange feeling from the very start, but how could I have known when my own wife didn't mention anything before???

The next morning was a hard one; no one in the house spoke to us, not even to the innocent baby who had no clue about what's going on. What kind of religion do they think they have? If they were true Christians, they would not act like this, not even close to this. The total irony was that my wife had a brother who was a drug addict and was jailed several times for that, and on top of that he had an illegitimate brat daughter who was the favorite grandchild of my wife's mother, even the drug addict son who was the last of her children was the favorite among them all, this favoritism was obvious to everyone. This was pissing me off, because if you want to show that you are a person of God and that you care about worshiping, then at least show some just in your treatment. Her youngest son stole many times from her to afford buying his drugs, yet it's all OK with her. That totally fits into her religion and beliefs and simply is acceptable. But when my wife goes to express herself as a matured woman who has her own family already becomes similar to an outcast. Damn, people sometimes are just so disgusting.

On the same day her elder brother who was also a total loser, expressed his opinion about religion making himself "Plato" with the few books he read centuries ago. Yet, what to do? We were living in their house and just had to go along. By that time they didn't know yet that we had money, they all thought we came from Jordan totally broke with nothing in our pockets, so enslaving us was simply all right to them.

After this incident, we started to go out rather than breathing the poisonous air in the house, but every going out was taking a chunk out from the money we had.

The house itself was really a disaster and very unhealthy, it was more like of a bunker style, wherein, you have to go down about 10-15 stairs below the street to reach the entrance to the wooden salon. Furthermore, the mice in the house were like part of their family, something beyond description. Honestly, I hated myself for this stupid move I made; I was not against coming to the Philippines, but I wasn't comfortable being with her family, since I already had a general idea from my previous visit. But I never thought that it would or could be that bad.

A few days passed by from the night my wife and her mom fought, and every day we were going out with Aladdin, we were also buying our own food from outside. This triggered the golden question to come out "do you have money?!" and so my wife answered, "we are not that broke, we are just OK." Here came the unexpected blast, "well, since that's the case, then you better pay for the electricity of the air condition that you are using in the room that we gave you" wow, really wow, can this old lady be any cheaper? My wife looked at me and translated what was said right then and there, so I answered her with a smile "sure, why not?" "Since we are consuming so much electricity, then by all means, let's pay." Indeed, who's hungry for money will stay hungry, when the electric bill came; they charged us more than half of the entire house bill. I was so disgusted being there, but I knew that we were not stable enough to move out and rent a house, the money I had wouldn't be enough to survive for a long time. And I didn't want to make the decision of moving out and then later having to return, I'd rather be in the streets than going through such a scenario. The humiliation we were in was more than enough already.

Our expenses were rising; my wife was having a very delicate pregnancy, in addition to that, she had to constantly visit her thyroid doctor. The lifetime medicine she had to take was just so expensive. Funny enough, her mom who owned a pharmacy was selling us the medicine rather than being of help. But again, it's all about money in the end.

The pressure was also rising because almost everyone told my wife to have an abortion, particularly her friends, they were saying that her pregnancy won't succeed and if it did the baby will be abnormal. They confused her with all their interfering, man oh man, what I had to handle was more than I expected. What I don't and will never understand is how these people have the nerves to interfere with someone's private life?! To add on the pressure my wife's mother was sarcastically telling her that all of this is happening to her because she changed her faith. What my wife had to cope with, hear and handle was really tremendous. Luckily, she was strong, and her faith was strong as well. She said it loud and clear "What God will give me I will accept, if my son is to be born abnormal, I will raise him as my normal son, I will not take his life away, it's not my place and it's my right to do so. I and my husband will take care of the situation without the help of anyone."

Basically that stand made the most shut the hell up, but of course from time to time we would hear some comments from here and there.

As the days passed by, things started to get a bit lighter, most especially that we already made up our minds to ignore all what is been thrown at us. And since we showed that we had enough money which didn't run out as fast as they expected, they basically adjusted their treatment. However, for me I knew that I would not be always able to be quiet, especially when it comes to my wife and son, and so I decided to make a move and try my luck by applying for my German citizenship through the German Embassy in Manila.

Early 2005 I flew from Cagayan De Oro City to Manila in order to submit all the needed documents to the embassy, wherein I had all my documents already translated and authenticated, it took me about 5 days to finish all the paperwork and the submission of payment. This move also took a big amount of money that I had for our survival in the Philippines, but I had to make that move for the sake of a better future. I was so much conscious about not losing my family again, it happened to me before, and I didn't want it to be repeated. That's why I was taking every risk that could move me forward for a possible better future.

When I returned from Manila, my wife was kind of upset having had to take care of Aladdin all by herself plus her delicate pregnancy, of course I did understand the situation, but I am just a very normal human being and not the legendary "Super Man" I can't be in more than one place at the same time. Since I didn't want to be an additional pressure on her and I didn't want to give the satisfaction to her family that we were having a fight, I apologized to her that it took me that long, but I also explained to her that it wasn't really in my hand. So that night I took care of Aladdin without having any rotation of duty, just for her to be happy and satisfied.

The next day my wife told me that she wanted to take a preparation course for the nursing exam NCLEX. Of course her wish was my demand, despite that our money was already flying away but I couldn't say no. Though I was already pressured with everything that we were facing, but honestly, I didn't want to give her family the slightest chance to enslave us or further humiliate us. I was going through a real hard time, I was able to handle her family so far, particularly her unfair mother because I knew we had enough money to take care of ourselves, and to shut them up when it comes to the house expenses, but my biggest fear was from the near future when the money runs out.

By almost March of 2005 I started to Panic, what we had left was not enough to cover the entire month of our son's milk, so what about the other expenses? Doctor's visits, medication, food and drinks and the high electricity bills we were always charged. So my wife said that she would work at the family's Pharmacy and earn some cash, as much as I hated the idea, but we had no choice. Meanwhile, I tried communicating with all the people I have known to help me out before we will be eaten alive by the gloating family who would love to see us down.

Of course I realized that I was their public enemy, in their mind it was me who took away from them a milking cow, that was always providing them with whatever they wanted without looking back at her own self, and my wife did it because she believed that it would make them love her, or rather she tried her best to be treated like her siblings or even just close to it. The more the situation became terrible due to the difference of religion, so her family and in particular her mother were constantly looking forward to our failure, so that they could throw it back on my wife's face, that all these failures and hardship happened because of the change she put herself into. Living in such a rotten environment was killing me second by second, but I just refused to give up.

My wife started working at the pharmacy but was really not comfortable with it, for one her pregnancy, and the second and main reason was that one of her sisters who actually was running the pharmacy was giving her real hard time. It only took her two weeks to make my wife quit working at the pharmacy. Meanwhile I didn't stop searching for means to get funded, at least something that could make us survive for another 6 months, most especially with the known coming up expenses.

Finally, I was able to get a hold of the ex-senator in Jordan; who helped us during my wife's thyroid operation, I explained to him our situation fully and completely, at first, he was hesitant and then asked me how I would return the amount? Of course knowing my situation I didn't give false promises, I was totally open and honest with him, I even told him that it will be a case of "pay when able" no timeframe or whatsoever. He totally admired my honesty and told me that he will try his best. With his words I had at least some hopes to hold unto. A few days later he called me up and asked me to provide him with a phone number belonging to one of my family members, I didn't ask why? I just complied with what he asked.

Surprisingly, the very next day my sister called me up and gave me the reference number of a money transfer via western union. The senator gave the money in cash to my family and asked them to send the amount to me. I really was so speechless most especially when I knew that the amount was a little over US$3,500. What a relief!!! I was so happy and so thankful to this very great man who extended his help without even asking anything in return. His kind of people is more than rare on planet earth.

I gave the news to my wife and she was also very relieved and happy, so we went together to claim the funds and we opened a joint account at a bank in the city. Of course this kind of news never remains unnoticed; with that the treatment of my so called in-laws became better again. Wow, what money can do!!! It's just so crazy how people can flip so fast when money is in question.

The days passed by and my wife's delivery date approached and on May 20, 2005 she gave birth to our second son "Amir". All thanks to our Lord, he was a healthy boy which in a way was a very big slap on the faces of all the people who advised to have an abortion. In fact you could've seen the disappointment on some of these faces. Some people are just so envious of the very little things that you may have.

Just a month after the birth of Amir my wife suggested again leaving for the USA to try her luck passing the NCLEX exam, of course this time the situation was much different from all the times before, we had two kids, we were living with a family who basically doesn't want us, or to be more specific doesn't want me, and on top of that my schooling, wherein I was studying at that time. So having the responsibility all by myself seemed to be just too much and tremendous. She on the other hand was convincing me that the USA is the right place for us to be a united family and that it's a country where there are no family members who could spoil our days, she also added that once the money that we received from Jordan is gone, we will be in a real hard situation and even if both of us would work in the Philippines, we would not be able to live the life we used to, nor would we be able to build any future. All what she mentioned was logic but being at her family's house and alone with the kids was just too much for me, it was too much to take in at that moment. Nevertheless, we explored all options and discussed for days until we finally reached to an agreement. Since it's for the sake of our family we have to make sacrifices and since she was the one with a 10 year multiple entry visa to the USA, she was the one who had a better chance in making our family's dream come true. So, we started searching for a babysitter who can speak well enough English to be our helper and at the same time to take care of our babies while I am out of the house. It was simply impossible to depend on my wife's family, if ever you ask any house member for the favor of taking care of the kids, we had to basically kiss their asses to hear the word "yes I'll do it" sometimes we even had to bribe them to stay a couple of hours with the kids while we had to go out. If that was the case while my wife was with me, how much more would it be if I was alone?!

After a couple of weeks we found a great babysitter, she was married yet with no kids and her husband was in another city finishing his studies, she really spoke well English and was indeed very polite.

By around July 2005 she started to work for us and lived in the same house with us, but nothing was for free, the family of my wife used her to make some errands for them as well, despite that she was hired for the sole purpose of taking care of our kids. But there was nothing that we could have done or even said, we were simply living in their house and therefore we had to simply shut up and go with the flow.

Now in order for us not to be financially crippled, my wife approached one of her brothers who basically was the best among them at that time and for a long time after, she requested him to pay for her ticket and promised him that she'll be paying him back as soon as she starts working. Based on that agreement she secured the expense for traveling, and as for her pocket money I had enough that would be of help to her. With this arrangement the clock started ticking and the time for her departure came closer. By September 2005, she left us, Aladdin was already a year and a half old and Amir was only 4 months old. With severe heartaches we said our goodbyes and a new unknown future was drawing itself. Our kids were still too young to understand what was going on, but there was basically no escape from this sacrifice that we had to make in order for a dream to come true.

This time my wife had better luck and found a job pretty quickly, she worked as a nanny basically, but also had to make some of the house chores; the pay was relatively good and besides that she also had plenty of free time which she used to review for her NCLEX exam. As for me and the kids we were basically waiting for the time to come to get out of the house we were living in; thank God that it only took us about 3 months to achieve that. By December 2005 we were finally out of that bunker house, away from the human parasites and moved to a nice, small subdivision away from the city center and its pollution.

With this, the scenario was clear; my wife became the breadwinner and had the responsibility to be the financial supporter and I was the dad and mom at the same time. Both of us had to make this sacrifice for a better future, yet, despite that fact I wasn't comfortable with this setup, it was more than hard for me to accept it, but the circumstances were simply drawing the path.

Now since we had a stable income, we were able to afford having another nanny, one was for Aladdin whom we already had, and the other one was for Amir, at least I had the peace of mind when I left the house for my schooling; I so much trusted the nannies compared to the trust that I had for my so called in laws.

By almost April of 2006, we were able to have a "VOIP" line which enabled us to call the USA and be called limitless. This has helped us keep in constant touch with my wife. She also had the chance to let her voice be heard by the kids since they basically didn't know her. It was hard on her for sure, but there were no better alternatives.

This was also the time she had finally passed her NCLEX exam after 6 or 7 attempts, the hard work had paid off. Not long after, she even got accepted at a hospital and started to work what she always wanted, she became an official licensed registered nurse. This opened the doors for her to become a legal resident of the United States after the hospital petitioned her. This had many good sides to it but also some downsides, the good part was that she was able to file a family petition for me and the kids after she received her green card, so we were a step closer towards our future plan, however, since she was newly employed she didn't have the chance to come back to visit us, in other words, she had to be away from us for a total of 2 straight years. Meanwhile I was trying my best to be the greatest father and mother for my kids, the only time I would be away from them was when I had to go to school or when I went to work, wherein, I started to teach "IELTS" at an English Academy. I wanted to have the sense that I am also participating in the expenses we had, but I was definitely not making any money that could have been compared with what she was making. So, it was more of a sense that I am doing something rather than nothing, simply because the topic of money was and will always be a very sensitive topic for me. Furthermore, I really had a tremendous hard time grasping the idea of being married yet single at the same time; the absence of my wife was harder than it could be possibly put into words. So, basically holding myself back from women was another tremendous challenge that my wife didn't even think about, she was basically only thinking about the financial aspect challenges.

Anyway, while I was schooling, I met a very nice, polite and very high class doctor at the hospital; she was amazingly friendly and very helpful during my hospital exposure. Oh yeah, I failed to mention that due to my extreme love for my wife I studied nursing aside from education. I wanted to be a nurse just like her; I wanted to undergo the same examination that she suffered from for so long. I wanted to be that man who's fully and totally with her.

This doctor was an amazing young lady whom I loved to hang around while at the hospital, I learned so much from her. One day I invited her for dinner, and she accepted; so after my hospital duty I went home, freshened up and went out again to meet up the doctor at an Italian restaurant downtown. She looked different from her appearance at the hospital; she was so extremely pretty that no one could expect her profession. Honestly, if I wasn't a married man, I would've gone a different direction, but I just couldn't. Despite that I had a wonderful time with this lady I told her that I am a married man and have kids, I just wanted to make things clear from the start before slipping into something. The love for my wife always protected me from doing something wrong, but sadly she never knew that. Anyway, it was kind of a surprise for the doctor and wondered why we had a date then? So I answered that I'd be honored to have her as a friend wherein my friends in this country were really very limited. Of course I am sure that if I was single, it would've been a different scenario, but that was just not the case. After a lovely evening we parted ways, but I knew that there was some kind of a disappointment from her due to my status. Well, I think that I just needed to have someone close to me to fill in the great gap that I had in my life without my wife by my side.

Our friendship grew with time and I really admired this person to the max, she was really an exception to all of the bad experiences I've encountered in the Philippines. Two of my classmates and the owner of the Academy where I worked at, and his wife were also topnotch people who are still my friends till this very day. So despite of so many disappointments with people, I still had a few who really were amazing and totally supportive.

This brings me to a quick story, where you could see the difference between the people who like you for who you are, and the people who just want to suck your blood out. One day my wife sent us from the USA a big box full of stuff for the kids and for me, this was a passion of hers, she really enjoyed doing this. Among the things she sent was some medication, vitamins and some personal stuff for her mom, which of course she asked me to have it delivered. When I did, the question was exactly this, "did she send a box?" so I answered with yes, then she replied, "and that's all she sent?" and I was like "Yes, everything that's for you is in here" and then she goes like "what about the others?" I answered politely that there was nothing for the others, why is she supposed to? Of course the old lady didn't like it and had a pouching mouth. So I excused myself since I was on my way to the hospital for duty and had to go. To these people everything was about gaining, it didn't matter how much the gain was, but the more the merrier of course. Bottom line, for as long as there was gaining, they were happy about it.

At the end of July 2006 I graduated from my nursing school and got myself ready to study for the NCLEX exam, though the difference between me and my wife was that she was an RN (Registered Nurse) and I was only an LPN (Licensed Practical Nurse), basically one step below her.

Anyway, my lovely wife was really supportive and sent me all the necessary books for the exam. I was studying as much I could, was going to work and of course was with my babies. It wasn't really an easy job taking care of so many things at the same time, most especially and most importantly the kids. By that time we discovered that Amir had slow psychomotor skills, and that required me to send him to a specialist doctor to treat him as early as possible, it was evident that it was due the nuclear medicine my wife had to take for her thyroid treatment.

Despite of all and everything I took the NCLEX exam very seriously and wanted to pass it in the shortest time possible, so I used to study at a place downtown called "The study zone" it was very quiet there, and only people who were serious about studying were going to that place. Of course it wasn't possible to study at home with the noise my kids were making while playing. So the best solution was to study outside for a few hours daily. I became a known customer to that place and almost all students became kind of close to me, I was also known for the reason that I was teaching IELTS to a few of them. One day after I finished studying and was about to go home, a nursing student who was my friend already went out with me; she was a very serious and studious girl, so I enjoyed teasing her when she was too serious. While walking on the street she hit me slightly on my head due to my teasing, it was like a natural reaction. My God, I barely arrived home and a whole different story reached to the USA already, my wife called me up and asked me "what's going on with you?" I was wondering of the question because it was totally different from the way she used to ask me, yet I answered her, "nothing much really, studying like crazy" but I was still curious about the way she asked me. Then she told me while laughing "are you being a playboy?" So that meant she wasn't taking the question seriously, yet she wanted an answer. I still didn't understand and asked back "playboy?" Why? What made you say that?" She replied that a friend of hers called her up and informed her that "there was a girl walking side by side with your husband and playing with his hair while walking" Damn, I was so mad and flared up, my wife tried to calm me down, but I was really so pissed and told her that if I wanted to be a playboy I could've simply done so and long time ago, besides why would I be exposing myself to the public if I wanted to have something discreet? Then I explained what really happened and how I got hit on the head due to my teasing. My wife was laughing at me and tried to smoothen the topic and make me relax, but I was just so mad about the fact how people try and do their best in this country to destroy the image of others and lie about everything. To a lot of people this is considered a proud achievement. This is truly so sad, because there is so much potential in the country and there are so many good people who get stepped over due to this kind of people who are simply rotten inside and outside. This incident gave me a new lesson on how to deal with people in the Philippines and to be more careful. What kept me hanging in there and gave me joy and happiness were my lovely kids, being around them was simply my whole life. Of course I had this inner pain from being away from my other kids in Jordan who were deprived of me due to their mother, but, there was just not much that I could do. By around January 2007 I flew to Hong Kong to take my NCLEX exam after I got myself registered with the "Public Health-State Board of Connecticut". This was my first experience with such kind of an exam; I studied almost 4 months preparing myself for this moment. The system of the exam is unique, the computer might shut off automatically at any point during the exam, it either means that the examinee made great and no need to continue, or the examinee made terrible and there was no point on asking further. With me it was a different case, the computer didn't shut down; it kept asking me until I finished the entire 205 questions, a total of 6 straight hours. That simply meant that I was doing OK at times and messed up at times, so the computer extended me to the maximum limit. By the time I finished the exam I was so drained out and very uncertain how I did? I called up my wife and told her what happened; she was an NCLEX expert already and was the best person to ask for an opinion. She was pretty thrilled and excited and told me that I had a good chance, but in the end we both had to wait for the results to come out. My total stay in Hong Kong was only 3 days and then I flew back to my babies whom I missed very much. About 2 weeks of waiting torture, the results were out already and available online, with fast beating heartbeats I entered my information into the system and here it was. "I flunked". Ahhh, that was so frustrating and so painful, I then realized the pain that my wife was going through when she had this kind of results. But I also learned from her personal experience not to give up, and with that I decided to retake the exam on April 2007, however, I changed my destination and booked my exam to be taken in Saipan-Northern Mariana Islands. This trip was more expensive than Hong Kong and the flight was also about 3 hours longer, so in order for me to save money I came up with the idea to ask if there was anyone among my study friends who would also take the exam in Saipan during the same timeframe, and indeed a very strange coincidence that the same girl whom I used to tease and hit me on my head while walking, was the one who booked for the exam. So, before making any commitment to the girl I asked my wife if it was OK with her that we'll be traveling together and even staying together to save on the expenses. I didn't want to be in another situation where I had to explain myself again. At first my wife was hesitant but when she knew how much the savings was, she agreed to it, since it was really a lot of savings. But of course, it wasn't an agreement without the constant reminder of having to be a "good, behaved man".

The more she kept reminding me with that, the more I got fearful from the entire trip already, it somehow had this negative effect on me, it just becomes annoying when you constantly have to hear the same. But then I decided to just concentrate on the main purpose of this whole trip "Passing the Exam"

And finally, the day had come, and we flew to Saipan, a beautiful Island and the largest in the Northern Mariana Islands, a commonwealth of the United States in the western Pacific Ocean.

So, I and my friend took a cab and drove straight to the hotel wherein, we were given a beautiful room with a balcony that had an ocean view. That alone was already an amazing start. I called up my wife immediately and informed her about our arrival. We probably spoke for about 15 minutes, had a good laugh as well and then she wished me to have a great time, pass my exam and to enjoy my one week stay in Saipan. I really appreciated that gesture wherein she somehow understood the negative effect she was causing me from constantly repeating the same.

We spent the first 2 days reviewing for the exam and the third day was the big day. The exam finally started. As soon as the first question popped my heart was in a marathon, so I had to take a deep breath and reminded myself that this is what I worked for so hard, it was all for the sake of my family, therefore, focusing should be my main objective at this point, in order to achieve my aim, to make myself, my wife and my kids proud of me. Indeed, I was so concentrated that I didn't even feel the time was passing until suddenly, my computer I was examining on shut off at question number 85, after only an hour from the start of the exam. That meant that either I messed up big time or I made really well. Answering 85 questions was the minimum required number of questions to be answered. I left the examining room and started recalling my experience in Hong Kong, there it was the total opposite, I reached the maximum number of 205 questions and spent a total of 6 hours behind the computer, with an end result of failing at that time, So I was totally dazzled about the extremes that have to happen in my life. Anyway, I just waited for my friend outside to finish her exam, and it was just 20 minutes' difference between us until she came out, So, since we both had no clue how we did, we decided to call our perspective families and just enjoy our remaining days in Saipan and wait for the results to be out, rather than burning ourselves thinking about something that we had no control over.

However, waiting for the official results to be out would totally drain a person, since it would take up to 6 weeks, so, since I experienced this before I knew that there was a way to get the results after 2-3 days via a website called "NCSBN" and paying for the service wasn't expensive either. And that's what happened, 2 days after our exam we logged online, paid for the service and the moment of truth was just a click away, I was hesitant to click because I didn't want to see a negative result, but there was no escape. So, I clicked, and the result is still flashing in front of my eyes "I PASSED". Whew what a relief, what a feeling and what a joy to see your hard work prosper!!! Now I was worried about my friend, I didn't want to be in such a joy without her, most especially that we spent a long time studying together. And luckily, she was a winner too. She called up her family and I did call my wife delivering the wonderful news. These happy moments could never be forgotten.

Fun days always pass fast, and the week was already over. We had to fly back to the Philippines. We kept in touch for quite some time after our return, but sometimes people just get too busy with life and their own problems and tend to disappear. And that's what happened to this friend. So, it seems that she was just a small chapter in a book, when the chapter ended her name was never mentioned again.

Days passed and I was just doing what I always did, taking care of my babies, the best job I've ever had. However, to be of help as much as I could for my wife who was away from us, I worked at an English center owned by an amazing couple. The owner used to be my English teacher during the time I was studying nursing and his wife taught me some "Bisayan" which is the language of the people living in the city of Cagayan De Oro. Despite that the income I earned was close to nothing compared to what my wife was earning as an RN in the USA, I continued to work to have the sense that I am at least doing something rather than just sitting at home.

From time to time I and my wife had to have some money arguments which always was a triggering point for me, it made me feel as if I was worthless. I should have been alarmed by then, but my positive thinking, my love for my wife and kids never made me think beyond the argument point. I took the pain from being deeply hurt and just moved on every time these issues arose.

That was one of the reasons I never stopped working despite that the money earned wasn't even worth it. On the other hand, the owners of the center were like family to me, and I always felt welcome there. They even encouraged me to take up my Diploma in TESOL (Teaching English to Speakers of Other Languages). I followed their advice and registered to a college in England on January 04, 2008, and thankfully my wife didn't make a fuss about the payment and even encouraged me to go for it. Now these beautiful gestures from her made me always forget the times she was mean and mindful about money in general. It made me believe that there is something very nice inside her despite the times she showed the total opposite.

Again, I wanted her to be proud of her husband and of his achievements, and so I studied very hard to finish my TESOL with a high grade in the shortest time possible. I was multitasking, taking care of the kids, working and studying at the same time. As much as I was pressured, I was contented, simply because I was doing it all for my family.

In 4 months I was done, on April 09, 2008 I got my Diploma in TESOL with an "A" Grade. An amazing feeling of achievement that made me proud and determined that I could do more. So, I applied for a part time teaching position in a Korean International School in the city in order to have an additional income to help out my wife. A few months later my wife came to visit us in the Philippines, and it so happened that she got pregnant during that short one month stay, though we only discovered that when she was back in the States again. As usual, whenever she comes to visit us in the Philippines a whole bunch of time is spent with her family, since it's "milking time". Not that I have anything against giving and sharing the blessings God gave us, but the feeling of being used was simply killing me, they were so shameless that one of her sisters asked for my wife's watch while saying goodbye at the airport, just imagine how low that is!!! And since my wife always wanted to be nice to them and basically was buying their love rather than having it given by them naturally, she took the watch of her wrist and gave it to her. Honestly, it pissed me off big time that my wife was just so naive and didn't want to see what her family was doing to her, despite that she knew that she was the milking cow. This family never cared that their daughter was sacrificing for her own family, being away from her husband and children to earn a decent income to prepare for a brighter future. They just cared about themselves and what they could get from her.

These kinds of issues caused us to be always in a sort of tension when they happen, but in order to let the ship sail, I had to let go of my disappointment and close my eyes towards this unfairness. I was just hoping that our petition to the USA will be out soon and that we would start a whole new chapter there without her family interfering in our personal life and without being used by anyone.

On July 09, 2009, my wife gave birth to our last son "Aziz" in California-USA. About a month later she came to visit us again and of course brought with her our newest member of the family who was added to the list of my responsibilities. Taking care of 2 was hard enough already, but now I had a third one. Thank God, I had helpers at home who were taking care of my babies while I had to be out of the house, otherwise I would have called it "Mission Impossible ".

Other than having a new member in the family is nothing worth mentioning, the rest was all the same, nothing changed. Whether it was her family's greed or the short stay of my wife, though this time she had about 15 days more. And as always, happy moments must pass fast, before you know it, time's up already.

Aziz was barely 2 and half months old when his mother had to leave him just as she left Aladdin and Amir before, but what to do? She had no choice, it's either this sacrifice on her part and mine or settle for what's much less with no possible future to be forecasted. The American dream was our goal and aim and therefore had to handle all the hardships and the long distance relationship. I never felt as if I was really married, it was like a part time marriage or even much less than part time. Despite that we were talking on the phone on almost a daily basis, but the distance was just there. Even the kids didn't know their mother really, if it wasn't for her almost daily calling, they probably wouldn't acknowledge her. I did all that was in my power to always keep mentioning her in front of them, because I knew that calling was never enough, her presence was simply lacking.

About a year later I came up with the idea of working for myself and open the same type of business which I was running in Jordan, fine engraving on fancy pendants. Now the obstacle was the startup capital for the business. I discussed the idea with my wife over the phone, and I could say that she was kind of encouraged but with some hesitations. As usual money was an issue. After several days, we spoke again and she suggested to borrow the money from her mother, wherein, she had inherited lands and is quite well off. As much as I hated the idea, I had no other choice if I really wanted to pursue with my plan, so I requested my wife to test the waters first before we go any further. Of course, my wife wasn't her other sisters, which only meant that there were conditions to be applied. The main objective was "gaining". So, a payment plan was set with interest of course. At this point I totally blame myself for going along with it. I thought that they would for once treat my wife "the milking cow" as they treat all the others, one of her sisters borrowed around 3 million Filipino pesos which is equivalent to about US$ 60,000 with no interest and no plan on how to pay back the money. Another sister of hers was running their family business which was a long existing pharmacy and managed to rob them for years without anyone noticing until the business almost collapsed from debts and unpaid checks. She stole more than 5 Million pesos, equivalent to

US$100,000, and what happened? Nothing, nothing at all, she didn't pay a single penny back and even stopped talking to her family. Was she ashamed? No, of course not, she was just pissed off why she got finally caught. One of her brothers was a drug addict as I mentioned before and stole from his mom and from the family tons of money for years, yet, with no consequences whatsoever. But when it came to my wife, she was treated as the black sheep of the family, despite that she was the most caring child, who always supported all members of her family with no exceptions.

I still blame myself till this very day, why have I accepted to borrow the needed amount from my so-called mother in law??? The amount was only about US$ 10,000, but since I knew that if the business picks up, I could return the amount in no time including all the interest she was asking for. And so, my business journey started, and I opened my kiosk inside a mall in the city of Cagayan De Oro in December of 2009.

The concept of my business was successful, and I made tremendous progress in a very short time. A progress that fired up an envy in the hearts of the family, they didn't have to say a word, you could simply feel it, it was just in the air. And Man, Oh Man, my mother in law kept coming to my store asking for money despite that I was paying the agreed upon monthly payments inclusive of the interest.

At times, I was hating myself for opening the business despite of the achieved success. Just imagine how it feels when all your hard work doesn't count for anything and that your success is only due to the borrowed amount of money which wasn't even given as help or support but given to make money out of you. That is exactly how my wife's family made it appear directly and indirectly. Several times I complained to my wife over the phone and informed her about how her mother who keeps coming to the store to "borrow" money. I used the term borrow here, because that is the term she used when she was asking for more. My wife was pissed and even told me not to give her mom anymore, but there were times when I just couldn't say no, especially when she was literally begging for it, and in front of my employees. I was embarrassed for her and didn't accept for an old lady to be in such a situation regardless of her unfairness. I am not a saint, but there are times when your heart controls rather than your mind.

Six months later I got two new partners, one from Turkey whom I've known from one of his visits to Cagayan De Oro to a Turkish family who were my neighbors. So, I wasn't really the only foreigner in the neighborhood, and that was kind of a relief for me. This Turkish family was truly amazing and made me feel as if I was one of them.

And the other partner was my Doctor friend whom I've known during my hospital exposure at the time of my nursing study. These 2 partners enabled me to open 2 further branches in the Metro Manila area. The start was amazing, and the people loved our items and the service of fine engraving. The only downside of the business was the rental inside the shopping malls was just way too ridiculously high. And on top of that I had to frequently fly from Cagayan De Oro city to Manila and stay there for a few days, which of course was an additional expense and a lot of hard work. Despite of the great reputation the business earned in a very short span of time, all these expenses combined and having money partners in the picture made the profit pretty low, but I didn't let that pull me down, on the contrary, I was determined to make this business as big as I could, and I even started to work on making a brand name. Short after, I offered my business for franchising which had a tremendous loud echo. All of these events happened during the first 10 months of the business's existence. Of course, I had my dry days, as it is the case with probably most businesses in the world, there are times when the business slows down, and the income barely covers the expenses. But, as long as the wheel is rolling there is nothing to worry about. As such was my case.

But what happened next is what no human brain can process, a blast from HELL that literally destroyed everything. The events that I am about to share will start sweet, but don't get deceived as it happened to me. Within a few months only, that sweetness turned into extreme bitterness and then into a fatal poison.

Here is the sweet part, after almost 6 years of waiting, sacrifice, pain and suffer, our petition to the USA finally came out. An unexpected timing, a time when I was working on expanding the business. But I didn't care about money, all I wanted was for us to be finally united and start to live together as one family, this is what we worked so hard for, waited so long and sacrificed so much. So, of course I prioritized and with no hesitation to sell the business and prepare for our move to the USA.

The process of selling wasn't easy at all, most especially that I had 3 branches and was asking for a decent amount of money because it was well worth it. These events found place in the beginning of 2011.

Several buyers were interested but didn't pay the amount I asked for, until a young businessman from a wealthy background and a known family approached me. We had several meetings and a lot of paperwork until the deal finally pushed through. Surprisingly, this young man was also looking for a piece of land to buy in a well-known area in Cagayan De Oro city, and I just had what he was looking for, my wife's mom had a land there and wanted to sell it a long time ago, yet she never found the right buyer. So, I offered him the land as well, after I spoke to my wife on the phone of course. The arrangements were made, and the agreements were signed.

Despite of all the aforementioned attributes he possessed, he gave me a hard time paying, most especially that I accepted checks which have constantly bounced after the 3rd month.

But if I didn't accept payments via checks, I would not have sold the business, and I needed to get everything ready for the move to the US. So, I had no choice really, and had to handle the pressure of following up his payments. Anyway, after a period of give and take I finally got all the money for the business, and the money for the land was given to my wife's mom. Of course, I didn't offer my client to my wife's family because I am an Angel, or because I just wanted to help, NO, helping time for me was no longer on the table for these people. I offered to sell their land to my client with the amount they asked for and had a profit on top of it. That move I made was with the complete knowledge of my wife. I got back all the extra amounts they made me pay in one way or the other. For me, it was fair and square.

I paid off all my debts and whatever I owed my partners and was ready for the next step.

The story gets even sweeter, I was so excited that everything was going into the right direction, and so I told my wife that I will be applying for a Visa to the USA and come to visit her along with our youngest son Aziz who was already an American citizen. She was so happy to hear the news and extremely excited. And indeed, my application was accepted at the American Embassy in Manila on October 25, 2011and I was granted a 5 years' multiple entry visa to the USA.

All that sounds so promising and sweet, right? When I called up my wife, she was so happy that I was granted a visa and even asked me what my plan was and when I would be coming to the States with Aziz.

I was so overwhelmed and happy that I just wanted to fly right then and there, but of course I had to arrange everything for my other two kids first, leaving them behind with the helpers in the house had to be organized and arranged.

About a week later, my wife surprised me with another wonderful news, she got notified for the eligibility of becoming an American citizen and she asked me what my opinion was regarding a change of name, and what was even more surprising, the name she chose was "Ayah". I was speechless and only told her that I would support her with whatever she wanted, for as long as it would make her happy. Then I added, when she's happy, I and our kids will surely be happy, and we can't wait till we are all united and start our lives as a real family, all under one roof.

Then we had a nice laugh over the phone, we were joking and talking as if there was no tomorrow.

Exactly two weeks later from that wonderful talk on the phone, there was the first blitz from hell that turned our lives upside down, particularly me.

My wife called me up at around 11 PM Philippine time, and she was extremely cold, as in so cold that it never ever happened during our entire relationship and marriage time. I didn't understand what the hell was going on. So I asked her what was wrong with her? If anyone at work bugged her? Or if she was not feeling well? I had like a million questions, totally worrying about her? But it was none of what I had asked, and then she suddenly said the following words "I want out".

I was like, huh? What are you talking about? She simply repeated the same words "I want out" and then added "I can't take it anymore". The more I was puzzled and asked "you want out what? And you can't take it anymore, what? what are you talking about?" And then she just started to pour a whole bunch of crap on me, it felt like as if I was hit by a train while sleep walking, I didn't grasp the nonsense she was talking. She threw accusations on me that I am hitting my babies on the head, and I was like "what the heck are you talking about? what nonsense is this?" and then she jumped 9 years back stating that I slapped her face that time. I was just in such a shock that I stood there like a total moron. So, I asked her "why are you bringing this up when it happened a one single time and 9 years ago? Something that I apologized for a trillion times, a topic that was closed and never reopened, something that you were the one who provoked me to the maximum limit when it happened. Why are you doing this?" But she never answered me, she was just pouring more and more until she reached the "money topic" and then said, "I am tired of sending you money, I work so hard for it" and again I was totally dazzled and had to answer her, "wasn't that what you wanted in the first place? Didn't we agree to exchange roles since you had the chance to travel to the US and find a job? Didn't you convince me over and over again that this is the best for us as a family? Didn't you mention that we both have to sacrifice in order to reach the desired goal? We both sacrificed big time, I am married but not really married, don't you know how hard this is? Don't you know how hard it is to be responsible for 3 hyper boys? Don't you know how many times I got tempted to fuck around but never did? Don't you know how hard it is to be a dad and a mom at the same time? Studying, working and taking care of the kids is nothing to you? I never told you that I am tired of doing all this as you are now whining about the money you are sending, which is our agreement and arrangement in the first place. And why would you feel such, when we already reached the end line of waiting? It is just a matter of a few months and we will be united after all these years, and I will be the one to work, day and night if I have to, I am even willing to pay you every single penny back that you have spent on us. If money is so damn important to you, you can have everything, I don't care about money and you should know that by now. So what is this fuss all about? Please tell me" And she simply answered, "I want a divorce."

There are no words to describe the feeling I had at that moment, my tears just went down without my knowledge, my shock was doubled, for one the words I heard and the other from not understanding what the hell was going on?! So, I made a whole bunch of obvious questions "Are you sedated? Are you in your full mind? What happened to you? Is there anything I said or have done wrong these past 2 weeks? It has just been 2 weeks that we were laughing and giggling and making jokes, and now this? No right mind can absorb this."

And guess what she answered? "I fell out of love". Wow, truly wow, can anything be more bullshit than this? We have been married for 9 years and have known each other for 11 years, have been through thick and thin and were waiting for the moment to be united, and now once it's there already she just destroys it all with 5 selfish words "I fell out of love"!!! No regards to the kids and their feelings, no regards to the extreme sacrifice we both put in, no regards to the time I spent in the Philippines trying my absolute best to be the best father and mother there is, trying my best to remain faithful. And while I was so focused on just being helpful to her, she was building her future and got all that she wanted and now she just turns her back as if nothing ever was between us? Is that even humane? Is that really normal?

The worst is still to come dear reader, that was just the start of hell's blast. My wife shamelessly told me for us to just be friends and to simply forget all that was between us. I couldn't handle all of this sudden nonsense and told her that we'll talk some other time, since this is just way too much bullshit to take in one dose.

That was a night full of nightmares, my mind was exploding, and my fear and anxiety were at their highest peak. I knew that there was something very fishy and rotten, no human could change like this for no damn reason. To be honest, I didn't know what to do? I was so lost, so down and so frustrated. With no sleep that night I went to my wife's family the next morning, hoping that they might have some humanity in them despite of their greed and hunger for money. I was in a situation where the saying of "A drowning person holds on to a straw" totally fits me.

They listened, yes, but I never could tell what was in their minds, they were showing a kind of sympathy, but I just couldn't believe it, my long experience with them made me cautious, but apparently not cautious enough as you will soon find out.

Basically, everyone in the family knew what happened, these types of news spread fast. But I was just trying to stay optimistic and was hoping that the storm will pass without actual damage. In the evening, I called up my wife again, but she didn't answer her phone, of course this whole new treatment made me worried sick, I was so afraid for my babies and the impact it will have on them. I needed to talk to someone so badly, I wanted to hear other people's opinion, so I called up a Jordanian friend who was also residing in the same city I was in. I told him the whole story from the past 2 weeks up to the point that happened last night. He was in shock as well and just couldn't believe that this is something natural. I was sinking deeper and deeper, and my thoughts were not stopping. My kids noticed me and without knowing what's happening, they just came to me and embraced me so tight. My tears were falling, and my heart was torn apart but I couldn't say a word. My kids told me these exact words "don't cry baba, everything will be OK". All I could do, was embracing them.

Later, at around 11.30 PM my wife called, and I simply asked her why she didn't answer her phone, she rudely replied, "I don't have to, besides, there is no talk between me and you except about the kids" The more she spoke the more I was convinced that this person couldn't possibly be my wife, there is something so wrong about all this. So I answered her "Alright, as you wish, but let's give this one final try, let me come to the US with Aziz and see maybe we could talk it over face to face, rather than on the phone, or are we not welcome?" She replied, "You can come if you want to, but don't expect anything from me and I am not paying a single penny, and just so that you know I won't take an off from work" I was just shaking my head and listening to all these hurtful words. Then I told her that I will take my chances, in the end I am not doing it for myself but for our kids.

On January 31, 2012, I sent my wife a very nice bouquet of flowers with a card which I have ordered from online shop, the occasion was our 9th wedding anniversary. Then I followed that bouquet with another one on the 13th of February 2012 with another card that had the following message to her "Happy Valentine's day honey, it's a day advanced cause I just wanted it to arrive before us. don't worry, I have no expectations whatsoever, all I want is to greet you and wish u all the best. always love u."

On the 13th of February, I arrived with Aziz to LA, it was around 11 PM and we both were so exhausted from the long flight. But guess what? All the people who were on the plane had someone to pick them up, except us, no one was there. I was so pissed off, mad and hurt. I called my wife and informed her that we are at the airport waiting for her, and she just answered "OK, just wait" It took her 45 minutes to arrive. What a shame!!!

What hurt me the most was that she didn't even bother about her little boy, if she had such a grudge on me for whatever unknown reason to me, what had this to do with this little 2 and half year-old boy? She was simply going too far.

When she finally arrived, she didn't come alone, she was with a female friend whom I heard about since less than 5 months ago. Back then, my wife told me that she has known someone and was telling me about her. But I didn't give any importance to that at that time. She was truly an ugly looking Filipino girl with extreme short hair just as my wife described her 5 months ago.

Anyway, my wife gave me a passive hug and then carried Aziz and kissed him, as if it's so cool and so fine to be late. And when we were about to get into the car, my wife refused for me to be in the front seat, she had this alibi that Aziz will be in the back seat and that I should be with him. I was pissed enough from waiting in the cold weather with Aziz and didn't have the will to open my mouth. So, the very beginning of this trip was so messed up already. Once we arrived the house, there were a bunch of Filipinos eating and drinking as if there was a party going on.

My wife's housemate was a close friend of hers whom I've also known since 2003 when I got married. In fact, she was the witness to our marriage. She greeted me and was happy to see me, probably much more than my changed wife. I excused myself and went to the room with Aziz, since we were so knocked out, and my wife stayed with the visitors. So sensitive, right?

When my wife finally came to the room, she brought in an air mattress and told me to sleep on the floor, and since Aziz refused to be with his mother, he slept with me. No talk whatsoever happened between us that night.

Aziz woke up a couple of times at night, wherein I had to feed him and change his diapers, and his mom was just sleeping, probably tired from the party they had in the house.

In the morning, it was Valentine's day and so I gave her my prepared gift and asked Aziz to tell his mom "Happy Valentine's Day Mama". She took the gift and said, "Thank you, but I don't have anything for you" And so I answered, "As I told you, I have no expectations, I just want this black cloud to pass by, not for me, but for our kids". She just shook her head and raised an eyebrow and said, "I'll make breakfast if you want to eat" Is that even questionable? But I just tried to remain cool and answered "sure, why not?"

Our first day in California, but we stayed in the house the whole day, she tried playing with Aziz, but he didn't get used to her yet, so he gave her some hard time which actually pissed her off. I explained to her that she shouldn't be like that, he is just a child and still new to the environment. She tried to make a fight out of this, but somehow, I managed to go around it. I was so deeply hurt, every second felt like a century of pain.

Her ugly female friend came and brought with her a gift for Aziz, then they started talking to each other in their language which made me take Aziz and go to the room. I played with my baby for a while and then he fell asleep. As for me, I was just on the air mattress thinking of what is going on? I was more lost than ever and had an aching heart, so aching that I thought that I would have a heart attack.

At night, I finally had the chance to talk to my wife, and I asked her to be open and honest with me, and she agreed to be. So my question was straight to the point "Is there anyone else in your life?" and she answered me "No".

So, of course I had to dig deeper, I just needed to know the truth, one way or the other. I asked her if there was anything that I have done or said wrong that made her have such a complete flip and made her a totally different person, a person whom I have not known before. Yet, she was just beating around the bush and kept telling me that she fell out of love, which of course didn't make any sense, why now? Why not when we were on the highest point of hardship? Why not when we were missing each other so much not knowing when the petition will be out? Why not when we were literally broke? And many other incidences.

How can this be? when all these hard times were already past us, we handled the worst situations ever, and now, after the petition is out and after she was about to become an American citizen, she fell out of love? Really?

Despite all that crap and bullshit, I didn't give up. I told her "If ever I have done anything consciously or unconsciously that made you hurt, I am apologizing for it. If ever I am to pay all the amounts of money you sent to us, I am willing to, even if I must work, day and night for it, and I will surely not deduct a single penny of what I have spent on the family before you started working, because that is simply my duty. I am willing to do all that it takes to save this family. I love you and I love our kids, so please don't throw all these years behind your back as if there was nothing between us." She replied, "why are you doing this?" Her answers were so immature and selfish, she was trying her best for me to just give up, without even giving me a straight and truthful answer. So, I replied "I am not doing anything aside from saving this family from being destroyed, my love for you is, was, and always will be genuine. We have three lovely Angels together; they deserve from us to handle whatever it takes to stay as one family."

Despite that she didn't like what I've said, but up to this point, we never called each other by our names, we used the term "honey" which gave me a slight hope that there might be something to work on. I was still optimistic despite of all the hurtful moments I was going through.

The next morning my wife went to work, and I stayed the whole day with Aziz alone in the apartment doing nothing. Just moments before she returned home, I was cleaning after Aziz, and it seems that I made a wrong body move which twisted my back and I fell on the ground not being able to move myself. It was a pain from hell, as if I didn't have enough! When she entered the house, and saw me on the ground, she told me "Is that a new game?" But, from pain I wasn't even able to answer her. With all the power I had in me, I crawled towards the bed because it was the closest to me, and I barely was able lay down, the pain was so severe that my tears fell. Then she realized that it wasn't a game as she accused. I requested some strong pain killers and water, and I apologized for any inconvenience I may have caused. She brought me the medicine and even helped me by holding the glass of water. But on the other hand, she was murmuring on how would she be able to go to work when I am unable to be with Aziz in such a condition?

I really didn't know what to answer her, isn't it an obvious thing for a parent to do, to have a few days off to be with her little child whom she didn't see for more than a year? If she had such a grudge on me, what had this to do with her son? I was simply going from one puzzle to another.

In the evening, her ugly friend came again, and my wife stayed with her for almost 4 straight hours without even checking on me for a single time. I badly needed to go to the bathroom but couldn't move a muscle, I was in an excruciating pain, and it was even more hurtful that I was treated so ugly from someone I have known for 11 long years.

When she came into the room, I couldn't hold myself back, I told her "what are you made of? Why are you like this? Don't consider me as your husband, and don't consider that you ever have loved me, and don't consider that we have kids together, wouldn't you consider a total stranger in need for help? You are a nurse for God's sakes, consider me a stranger who needs your help as a nurse, or is that even too much to ask? Don't you have enough time to spend with your new friend who is living in the USA, that you must spend so much time with her while we are here for you? Common, it's true that I told you I am not expecting anything from you and that I am taking my chances, but not to the extent of being treated like trash, you don't even have 2 minutes' time to check on me or even talk to me?" And she answered, "there is nothing to talk to you about, but there is much to talk to her".

Speechless, but I still needed her help to go the bathroom, so with complete humiliation I asked her to help me. As much as I hated the feeling, but when you have no choice, you got to do what you got to do. Yes, she helped me to get there, and she waited to get me back on the bed, she even let me sleep there rather than on the air-bed. Despite all her cruelty she had some simple gestures that made me hang in there, or that's how I was convincing myself. The next day, my wife brought with her some injections and some heat pads which helped reducing my physical pain.

It took me 5 days to recover, so, my first week with Aziz in California had been a disaster, there was nothing happy about this trip at all.

The day that I was walking again I received another slap on my face, my wife for the first time called me by my name and didn't use the word "honey" and when she saw me in another shock, she said "you better get used to it".

In the evening, I opened up the topic with her, and luckily, she had a slip of the tongue when she told me loud and clear that it was her ugly friend who told her that it doesn't make sense to call me honey if she is determined to finish the relationship with me. So, I knew that my wife has been BRAIN WASHED and God knows for how long? At least now I knew where the leak is coming from, but I still didn't know why and how? At night, I texted that ugly friend and told her NOT to interfere in the relationship between me and my wife, and that I knew it was her behind the suggestion of not saying the word "honey" to me. I also mentioned to her that if she really was my wife's friend as she claims, she should have been neutral if she has nothing positive to say.

The next morning, my wife just fired up and started shouting at me, asking me why I have texted that ugly friend, and that she had nothing to do with it. She added, that if she wanted to call me "honey" that no opinion of any person would bother her, and that she just wanted to stop using it. Of course, I wasn't born yesterday, I knew she was lying, I knew that there was something very wrong, but still doubtful, I still wanted to give the benefit of the doubt. This time I shouted back and explained to her that she has been played and manipulated, and that she had to be careful, because she was destroying everything we built.

However, she just didn't give a damn of what I said and told me to stay away from her friend. The argument was useless, and I had to change my method. So, I told her that it was my right to talk to her ugly friend for me to have the peace of mind.

Surprisingly, she agreed and told me to come along when she will have her naturalization ceremony the next day, wherein, that ugly beast was of course to be there. And so it was, the next day we went for that ceremony. While my wife was busy with the process, I was alone with her devilish friend along with Aziz, and so I had to be sure of my doubts and asked her with a straight question "What is my wife to you? What does she mean to you?" and she replied, "She's my friend and I will support her with whatever she does" so I asked "And does that include for you to encourage her to destroy her family which she sacrificed so much for up to this point? Aren't you supposed to be a good friend? You are a married woman as I understood, do you allow anyone to interfere in the relationship with your husband?" She gave me a yellow smile and said, "I don't care about my husband, I only got married to him to get the green card, and regarding the one you call your wife, she can do whatever she wants, and I'll advise you to back out."

What a shameless ugly devilish whore?! Excuse my language dear reader, but this is the simplest word I could use for such a low life person. I was so pissed off and mad but, couldn't show any of these emotions. I asked her politely "back off? And who are you to tell me such? This is my family which I will fight for, for as long as I breathe" And she answered me "Good luck with that". Wow, I truly didn't understand where she got all that confidence from? What was her game plan? How was she able to control my wife like that? A thousand questions popped in front of my face.

When my wife came out, I congratulated her and still behaved as a gentleman, but I was boiling from the inside. Just a few minutes later, the phone of that ugly beast rang, and it was her husband asking where she was? And she answered him that she had to spend some extra hours at work. She was so simply lying and guilt free in front of us.

when we arrived the house, I told my wife that after our son goes to sleep, I have to talk to her urgently. At around 10 PM I finally was able to sit down with her and told her everything that happened between me and her alleged friend, I even begged her to open her eyes and to understand that what she was doing was wrong, I even reminded her that this woman is a liar and doesn't care for her own family, how would she care for hers? But none of my words were heard.

When I found myself in such a situation, the next day, I called up the husband of that ugly devil and asked him if he could come by to pick me up, to have a coffee somewhere. Indeed, the guy was a real gentleman and after he was done with his work, he came to pick me up and we went out. Opening such a topic wasn't easy for me, especially to a guy whom I have known for less than 10 days. So, I told him that I wanted to verbalize to someone and that I was hoping for his kind understanding. I gave him a brief summary about my marriage life until the recent events, and then I expanded about his wife and her lies and backstabbing. Maybe what I've done was wrong, but I was just exploding from my controlled anger, I hated how this ugly devil was playing games on multiple fronts. I wanted him to let his wife stay away from mine, because I was so damn sure already that she was the one behind all this mess in our lives.

Late in the evening, when I went home, I called up the airlines and changed my flight date along with Aziz. We were supposed to stay for a month, but it was cut short to 15 days. It didn't make any sense to be more humiliated than this.

As a one last try to approach my wife and putting some sense into her, I wrote her a letter through my iPad, since talking was just off the table with this woman. The letter that I wrote was the following:

"I know that nothing I say is believable to you anymore or even makes sense, and I also believe that this writing will not make you realize anything, but then since I am on the edge of the cliff already, I will just go ahead and write this anyway, cause, who knows? Maybe a word of all this long writing will still make you open your eyes a bit.

It seems like you got manipulated big time and in a very smooth way, don't worry, you are not the only one, I fell for it as well, I really thought that your new friend is a good caring friend, straight forward and honest, but after analyzing, I came to the conclusion that I am totally wrong. I don't want to be judgmental, but this is my life and family that is affected here, and, therefore, I do have the full right to say this.

Now, please let me explain what I mean, you had that certain anger at me, frustrated and pissed even, for reasons that I don't even know why or how? Anyway, your so called friend takes the chance and talks to you, listens to you, but uses your being down and throws words at you in a very smart way, making it sound very caring and talking for your benefit, but it's like poison, making you more distant and more determined. How do I know that? In the evening of our big fight, your so called friend called me up and stated, that when she talked to you before, she kept asking you, if you are really sure of what you want, and that you kept saying that you want to end this, and then she added that I SHOULD LET YOU FACE THE CONSEQUENCES of what you are deciding without blaming her friends, referring to herself. And with regards to the word "honey" she stated that she's not sorry about it, and that she would not change anything what she said to you.

How did she manipulate me? I am down already, I am hurt, I am feeling that the world is collapsing on my head, and the stupid me, I allowed her to get inside my head, which made me determined on booking my ticket earlier, wherein, the thought was actually floating in my head.

Why do you think that she can hide from her husband the truth about being out with you, and further lie to him by stating that she's at work; it's simply because she's nothing more than a liar. This is not about her, but I am just pointing out to you what she really is and what I have learned and discovered in just a few simple meetings and encounters with her, so please open your mind for just a little bit without being mad and sour at me for reasons that I don't even know.

Look, I know that you have your own mind and make your own decisions, I know that you are a grown up woman and can take care of yourself, and others even, but at times like this, decisions can be so cloudy when you surrender yourself to someone manipulative who knows how to play with words and twist them in a fabulous good sounding manner, making your anger and accumulated bad thoughts aggravate, leading into a much bigger problem, like the one you are in right now "falling out of love".

I am using this last opportunity before leaving, to say what I see and realized and actually believe in, because after that I will no longer bug you with any text messages, letters, emails or phone calls, I will just text you or call you back if you approach me.

So, since this is my last hope of trying to make you see what you can't see, I am putting it all on the table, for once and for all.

How many times have I pointed things out to you in the past, things that you couldn't see nor did you believe in, and they all turned out the way I mentioned them to you, and every time your reaction was just a smile and you would say "shhhhhh" for me not to say anything, I am sure you can remember some of the many incidences that prove what I am writing you here.

Whether you believe me or not, that's up to you, but I always did my best for you and our kids, I did my best to work things out, to the extent of even being annoying, like I am right now by not letting go, but how could I, when nothing makes any sense, and the simple truth is that I truly love you inspite of being in so much pain from what's going on.

All I am asking is for you to give yourself the chance to look for the tiniest trace of love without being manipulated by anyone, and if it is still not there, then there is nothing that I can do anymore. In the end, you are the judge and the jury here."

But of course, the ship didn't sail smoothly, my wife was big time pissed off, the letter that I wrote was similar to toilette paper to her. And since arguments didn't help anyway, I preferred not to discuss anything.

But the non-discussion method didn't help much, just right the next morning my wife was bitching again on how I dared to open the topic with her alleged friend's husband. And so, I flared up, I couldn't hold myself back anymore. I shouted and cried at the same time and said, "You are so selfish, you defend an ugly beast whom you barely have known, a person who constantly lies in front of your face and you refuse to see it, you are destroying your own family with your bare hands and for what?" All the sacrifices mean nothing to you? Are you that blind now?" And she answered, "What have you done? Changing diapers?" WOW, she was so mean, she was so rude and cruel, NOTHING was acknowledged, to her, all I've done was the changing of diapers!!!!!!!

So, I shook my head and told her that I will be staying the remaining 3 days in a hotel and if she can't take an off from the hospital, I will just take Aziz with me. And she started threatening me, that she would go to the police if I took Aziz. I was like "Are you insane? Are you that stupid already that you can't even understand what's being said? If you want to go to the police, then by all means, go ahead, what will you tell them? My husband who came all the way from the Philippines for me and brought our son with him is going to a hotel because all I do is bitching in the house? Go, go ahead honey."

I took off my wedding ring and gave it to her and said "since my lovely wife wants to call the police on her husband for no damn reason, what is left? then I added "If you can take an off from work then be with Aziz, and if you can't I can take him, is this clear enough for you? She replied, "I will stay with Aziz". And so, I packed my things and left the house.

Did she bother where I'll be? Did she bother that I gave her my ring? Not at all, she was just a completely different person, someone I haven't known at all.

I called up one of her sisters who was basically the best among my wife's siblings, she was residing in Tennessee and married to an American. I told her all that happened and in details, she was speechless and didn't know what to answer me. No one was able to help. I was totally alone and helpless.

The 3 days passed and the day of leaving the US was there, so I called up my estranged wife and requested her to fetch Aziz to the airport and gave her the flight details. This woman was so mean already that she didn't even bother to offer a ride. But I didn't get surprised. I just called a cab and got my own ride.

At the airport, I still said goodbye to her and told her that I will call her up once we arrive.

From inside the airport after we were through with the security checks, I called up my wife. My voice was barely out, as if I was choked. I told her "Thank you for your hospitality and thank you for spending a few days with your son. No matter what you have against me, the kids have nothing to do it with it. So at least, think it over and find a way for the kids not to be affected. I tried to open your eyes, but you refused. Don't be mad at me, I just did what any caring father and loving husband would do." She didn't answer back, she was just crying.

I felt so sorry for my little baby who definitely was able to sense what was going on, I also felt sorry for my wife who was manipulated and big time controlled, but she was no little girl, she was a grown up lady who had experienced so much in life, she should have been able to distinguish between what's right and wrong, between what's good and bad, but she was just simply blinded and chose to destroy her own family.

When we arrived back to the Philippines, I called her up, just to inform her, but she was just as cold as the north and south pole combined.

A few days later she called me up and said those exact words "There will be changes from now on, I will be sending the kids money to my mom, and you will get it from her" I started laughing and told her "Keep your money to yourself, I will never play your dirty game and I will never let you humiliate me again" All of sudden, this filthy family of hers became her best friends, she trusts them and can even depend on them! I knew that she was cooking something, I just didn't know what.

I really had a very bad feeling, something was telling me that she is up to something, I just couldn't figure out what, besides, I really didn't want to think too bad of her, she has been with me through thick and thin for so many years, so, why now? I just had so many different thoughts crossing my mind, but I never was able to reach anything definite, yeah, how can any human being reach a definite conclusion when the outcome was far away from being humane???

In April 2012, less than a couple of months since my return to the Philippines, my so called wife rang me up to tell me that she was coming to the Philippines on April 18, and that she doesn't want to see me at first, only the kids, therefore, I should send them with her brother to Manila, where she will be staying with them for some time before coming to Cagayan De Oro city. At first, I said no, because I just don't trust her family, and secondly because the request was very odd, it just didn't make any sense, however, I was still trying to look at the bright side and was hoping that if I do accommodate her request, maybe and only maybe things will turn out to be OK, maybe it's alright for the kids to be with their mom and have some alone time, but I was NEVER so WRONG, I committed the biggest mistake of my life by finally agreeing for the kids to go to Manila under the condition that they will not stay for longer than 3 days; as much as I blame myself, as much as I know that it was impossible for me to figure it out, and even believe that the worst could happen, I truly can't grasp the idea nor can I believe that there was so much EVIL in her, till this day I am in shock, I can't believe that it happened, I can't believe that the woman that I loved from the bottom of my heart could have so much evil in her. This woman, this so called mother of 3 lovely children who had no clue of parenting, who had no closeness to them, decided to fully deprive them from their father who raised and took care of them and deprive their father from them, she literally KIDNAPPED the children.

The uncle of the kids came to pick them up from the house in order to go to the airport and escort them to Manila, I hugged them, kissed them and wished them to have a good time with their mom, not knowing that I was saying the most painful goodbye ever.

Later that night I called up my wife's number, but she didn't answer, so I texted her, but she still didn't reply, then I called up her brother who fetched the kids, and only after several attempts, he answered my call, and said "don't call anymore" I was like "excuse me?" I want to talk to my kids, but apparently it was all a game they played together, and they didn't let me talk to my kids, that's when I understood that I fell for their trap.

I still waited for the 3 days to lapse, since that was the agreement, but the results were still the same, so I knew that it was war on multiple fronts. The next day I went to 2 attorneys who worked together as a team and I explained in detail what had happened, and with that I filed a kidnapping case against my wife and her brother.

Of course, when they received the letter from the prosecutor's office, they quicky counteracted, and she filed a protection case against me, stating that I am a violent person and that I hit my children brutally, it's funny how the law can be manipulated, when in the first place she doesn't even live with us to make such a claim, and secondly, if that was really the case, why did she shut up all these years letting such a thing happen without even making a move? What kind of a person are you for God's sake?

Anyway, since my filed case against them was a criminal case, and since I am the foreigner living in their country, and since I have no connections as they do, the process was going slower that a snail, however, her case was accommodated right away and a court hearing was scheduled in a matter of days, how is that not possible, when her uncle is a retired judge and lives pretty close to the court where the claim was filed?! It doesn't take a genius to fill in the blanks, does it?

To add more spices to the filthy cooking, the landlord of the house where I and the kids were living at, came and told me that she was approached by my wife and her family asking her to kick me out of the house and demanding her to pay the deposit back, since my wife will no longer pay the rent, so, I smiled and told the landlord "I have been the one paying the rent to you ever since we moved to your house, right?" and she replied with a "yes", then I added, "if I will reach to the point that I won't be able to pay my dues anymore, that's the time legal actions can be taken, but not before, furthermore, the contract of the house is under my name and not theirs, and the deposit is not theirs, since they are not the ones living in the house, so, please correct me if I am wrong" The landlord immediately agreed with what I told her and said "don't worry, I am with you and not with them, I am just delivering to you what had happened and I hope that this problem will be resolved somehow."

Of course at that point, nothing surprised me anymore, I was not in shock nor was I furious about this low life move, I was already facing the worst and still had no clue where the path will end, and so, all the additional problems were just simple add-ons.

On the day of the court hearing, here it was, surprise, surprise, my so called wife the kidnapper, and guess who? Her girlfriend Ms. ugly face, both holding hands celebrating their sweet victory over 3 innocent children who didn't know what the hell was going on nor did they know where their father has been since the day that they left the house, what a shame!

Despite that my 2 attorneys presented my case with all solid evidence and despite my witnesses, such as the kids nannies, my neighbors and everyone who was close to me and saw me with the kids over and over again, the court decided to grant the protection based on no evidence whatsoever, but what can you say? When the officials are corrupted and bribery isn't off the table, then expect the unexpected.

Of course with the court's decision, their attorney used my kids forced presence in the house of my filthy in-laws as a legal action to further counteract the criminal case filed by me against them, and not only that, but they also followed it with a custody case. What made everything so disgusting and so obvious that the whole thing was perfectly cooked, was when the case was still ongoing, my so called wife was not even in the Philippines anymore, she left back to the USA with her beloved ugly-face girlfriend, leaving her kids at her family's house fully depriving them from their father who raised them all these years on his own. Despite that the court knew that, and despite that everything was crystal clear to them, and despite that I presented all possible evidence, from witnesses to documents to receipts, nothing was taken into consideration, I was simply invisible to them, and my attorneys were not able to do anything, they were also so frustrated from the obvious rotten officials, that they decided to give up on being attorneys, later I discovered that they were threatened. Of course this made me look for a stronger attorney who had his reputation, but at the same time who was extremely expensive. I had no options though, I had to fight this through, for the sake of my kids whom I have not seen nor heard their voices for a few months already.

I was literally dying every day, my heart was shattered, my mind was in a hurricane state, my thoughts were constantly on the move, my emotions were mixed between disbelief, anger, frustration, sadness, madness and everything that you could think of.

All these events happened, and my filed case was still under investigation, oh my God, things were just moving too slow, the case only moved forward after I hired the new attorney, he had guts and didn't fear anyone, but again, everything comes with a price. Anyway, by November 2012, the prosecutor's office issued a warrant of arrest against my wife and her brother by finding probable cause for kidnapping, however, by that time the court already gave sole custody to the absent mother, how could things become any more ridiculous?! Of course, I went right away to the court of appeal and appealed the court's decision, at least I should have better chances there, since there should be no direct influence and manipulation as it was the case at the regular court.

The arrest never took place of course, since the mother was in the USA anyway, and the brother became by the power of the corrupted officials the legal guardian of the kids, just imagine that!!! But does it end here? No, of course not, the criminal case that I filed and waited for half a year to be decided upon by the city prosecutor's office, never found the light at court, as soon as it landed there, it was dismissed, and the probable cause was thrown in the trash. So, in other words, I was just another "Don Quixote" fighting with the windmills, the only difference was that my kids were the ones at stake. No mercy and no sympathy from anyone, not even from their so called mother.

What made things even worse, I was given supervised visit rights once a week at the bunker house, they got away with their crime and I am the one being punished?! Really? Is that now how justice is being served?

The first time I saw my kids after many months, my tears fell like a waterfall, and my hatred for this filthy, rotten, stinky family spiked, I was determined to keep fighting until I have no power anymore; most especially when I noticed how my kids have changed, they were big time manipulated and I could sense the fear they were having, they were no longer the kids that I have raised.

Right after my first visit which was tremendously painful, I went to my attorney and explained to him what happened, and I requested him to find me any alternative way to have my problems resolved, since depending on the courts that are in the city is useless and it was evident more than once.

From that point on I made a new move, a move that was impossible for them to counteract, because I filed a case in the Islamic court in a city that was about 3 hours' drive away, so they had no connections there and no way to bribe anyone either, and on top of that, no one had the real love for their sister to drive a total of 6 hours back and forth to check what is going on. These people were at their comfort zone, knowing all the officials around them through their uncle who was retired judge as I previously mentioned, and there was more, one brother was working with the city hall, which meant very close connection to the Mayor of the city and other important officials, and the other brother also was working with the city hall and had his connections as well.

I explained to the Judge everything that happened with me and my kids, as well as the environment where my kids were at, and on top of that the absence of their so called mother who was given custody while she was not even around, furthermore, I explained that I filed a case in the court of appeal regarding that matter. So, I was advised to file for a divorce and to wait for the legal period to pass, this process took about 3 months, since there was mailing and waiting for responses.

Finally on January 04, 2013 the court issued a judgement and a certificate of finality that granted the divorce as well as the custody of my 3 children since the mother is absent and not in the country anyway. Then the court further issued a Writ of Execution wherein, the children had to be returned to me from the place they have forcefully been living at for almost a year already.

Knowing my ex-in laws and their influence as well as their capabilities, I had to be very careful, so, on Saturday, February 2, 2013 I made my regular weekly visit and once I was at the house and spent about 10 minutes with them, the court officers and police came and handed me the kids in front of all the household members who were present that morning, this came as a shock to them and they tried to fight and prevent me from taking the kids. However, I immediately took the kids and had a car ready to take us out of the city. It was so NERVE racking, and I wouldn't have made it without 2 friends of mine who backed me up and helped me all the way.

My kids were so happy, they hugged me and kissed me, they were in a state of total disbelief, honestly, this feeling can't be described with words. Though I knew that I can't be safe with the kids unless I am fully out of the Philippines, and therefore, I asked the driver to take us to the airport in order to fly directly to Manila, and from there to Jordan, wherein, I already had the tickets booked for the following day, however, prior to reaching the airport, I saw from a distance that some of my ex-in laws had a bunch of police with them, waiting for me to show up, so, I changed the plan and requested the driver to drive us to a different city, which was almost 6 hours away, but, I just didn't want to take any risks, despite that I had all the legal documentations necessary.

It was a very long and tiring trip; we spent the night at a cheap hostel and early in the morning we drove to the airport in order to fly to Manila. The luggage that I had was too heavy and I had to pay a lot for excess weight, but I didn't mind, I just wanted to have this nightmare behind my back already, at least that was my hope and aim.

Having had this amazing reunion with my kids was above all and everything, I just felt that all the hard time that I have been through was finally to be over and justice was finally served, but, unfortunately I jumped into fast conclusions and I should have known better, that these filthy in laws had a milking cow who was spending and supporting the needed briberies to make lawful acts unlawful, and to make the right wrong, and simply twisting everything around.

While I was waiting with my kids for the airline counter to open, a few men approached us having a picture of me and my kids in their hands, and they introduced themselves as airport security, then I was asked to present an ID, so, since it was really strange, I asked them politely what was going on! and they asked me to follow them along with my kids to the NBI (National Bureau of Investigation) office at the airport, but since the counter was about to open, I told them that I have a plane to catch; they replied that it shouldn't take long. Well, I believed what I was told or rather, I was confident that there is nothing I've done wrong, since I have all the legal authenticated documents needed. Inside the office an NBI officer asked where I was going and what right do I have to take the kids with me? So, with all confidence I presented him with the court order of custody with the finality certification, as well as the court's Writ of Execution, I also presented a printed copy of the Philippine's law requirements when a single parent wants to leave the country, at that moment the old witch sister of my ex-wife enters the room along with one of her brothers. Honestly, it wasn't a surprise, but what really surprised me was what happened next, the NBI officer told me that I have a custody order, but that they also have one, so I explained to him that they don't have any final decision and that there was still an ongoing case at the court of appeal regarding their document, however, his response was that I have to be at the NBI headquarter in Manila for that night, which simply meant that they wanted me to miss the flight. Then with a low voice he said the following "either you go peacefully, or we will do it our way" so, I was like, excuse me? Are you threatening me? I immediately called my attorney to let him know as well as my Jordanian friend in Cagayan De Oro, just to have some people know in case things get worse. My attorney advised me to go along, in the end, they will be responsible to reimburse the flight expenses. Based on my attorneys advice, I agreed to go with them, for as long as my kids are with me, but what happened next was just beyond description, we were already outside the airport's building, my two elder sons were holding my shirt from both sides, and my youngest was between my arms embracing me tight, then, one of the officers took my two elder sons away by force, and another officer tried to get my youngest off my arms by force as well, of course I held tight unto my son and so did he while crying so loud, then the officer stepped on my foot and shouted "let go, you are wanted for kidnapping", and that scene was in front of at least 500 people, my kids were shouting, crying and calling my name, they were literally freaking out, suddenly, my eyes fell on the 2 siblings of my ex-wife who were laughing about all what was happening.

I truly have no words that possibly could express the severity of what had happened, the way the 2 savage siblings were enjoying the emotional torture of my kids and the physical abuse of taking my kids away by force while stepping on my foot and twisting my arms, forcing me into their car, is just simply beyond description, a complete violation to human rights while totally disregarding the law.

Inside the car one of the officers was still twisting my arm, so, I told him, "you can let go already, you are 3 big guys, and I am alone, besides, my kids are no longer with me, so why are you hurting me by twisting my arm?" Eventually he let go, and I called up my attorney and told him what happened, and that they were taking me to the NBI's headquarters, so, he flared up and told me to give the phone to one of the officers, but they refused to talk to him, then the attorney told me to tell them that this will reach the president's office, which I did, and there faces couldn't be translated, but they swallowed it and took my phone away.

When we reached the headquarters, they took me to their offices and let me sit on a chair. Their task was accomplished, and now some other guy took over. He started questioning me and I started to answer all what he wanted to know. About an hour later, a guy and girl came to the office and they introduced themselves to be from the family's welfare office, and their question was about how I treat my kids? So, I understood that my filthy ex-in laws tried to play dirty again and twisting things around, they tried to question my fatherhood and credibility, but I had many evidence to counteract the lies, so I opened my iPad for them and showed them many videos that were taken without my kids' knowledge, it was very obvious for them that the accusations were all lies, they shook their heads and told me exactly these words "May the Lord be with you Sir". I asked about my kids, and they said that they were safe with them, but, if the case will not be resolved, then they will have to hand them over to my ex-wife's family. I just had a very deep sigh and didn't know what to say anymore; I honestly wished to die that very moment. But, hey. why that rush? There is still a bigger surprise my man; about 30 minutes after the people from the family's welfare office left, another guy who was an attorney came in and gave me his card, he said that he was sent by someone that I never heard of, strange, right? Well, it even gets stranger, he asked me about a few information, and then he said, "how much money do you have?" So, I told him that I had about US$ 200 left with me, and asked why? Then he smiled and said "look, I will be straight forward with you, if you can come up with1,000,000 Pesos (equivalent to US$25,000) then I guarantee you to get on the next plane with your kids" and then he added "it's all about who pays more" apparently, these filthy savages ex-in laws paid about $5,000 of bribery to make this scenario. With tears in my eyes, I shook my head and said "I swear if I had that money I wouldn't care about it, I would give it to you, and fight my filthy ex-in laws back, even if I am against it" He tapped my shoulder and said "I am sorry, but that's the only way, I hope things will work out for you, since you will be sent back to Cagayan De Oro city and handled by the local NBI office". After that he left and I stayed up the whole night at the office area, the officers who had the night shift were actually nice and

144

they knew that it was all fabricated, but they couldn't do anything, the only thing they did was giving my phone back.

I called up my Jordanian friend in Cagayan De Oro city and told him about my whereabouts, I also called up my family in Jordan who had no idea about what was happening with me. Of course, I knew from the night shift officers that they will fly me the next morning to Cagayan De Oro city and that I will be sent to the prosecutor's office at once.

The next morning I was escorted by two NBI officers and once we reached the airport in Cagayan De Oro city, I accidentally pumped into my Turkish neighbor who knew everything about my case, and he approached the officers and told them that, what they were doing is against the law, yet covering it up under the name of law, what an irony? They asked him who he was, and so he got is UN international police ID out, yet they didn't really give a damn and just continued their way.

The officers took me to the court building and then I was taken to one of the prosecutor's offices. She was really rude and told me that she will see to it to give me the maximum penalty and that I will be spending the night in jail until the court hearing the next day. So I answered her "don't you think that it's very strange that when I was the first to file a kidnapping case against my so-called wife and her brother, a case that took the prosecutor eleven months to give me a probable cause and nothing had happened afterward? and when I got my children the legal way through a court order I am being set up and now you are setting a court hearing right the next day and even threatening me with the maximum penalty? If courts have no respect for each other's decisions, then what kind of law is being implemented here? She stared at me with a mean face and said, "you'll find out tomorrow".

When I got out of her office escorted by a policeman, I called up my attorney and my Jordanian friend and asked them to do what needed to be done.

I stayed at the police station that night, but thankfully not behind bars, the police officer ordered the policeman to let me stay in his office after he heard my story. I was really impressed by their nice treatment.

Meanwhile, my friend and my attorney made their efforts and informed many different parties, such as the Ministry of Foreign Affairs in Jordan, as well as The Jordanian Consulate in Manila and The Jordanian Embassy in Japan, furthermore, and that was the big surprise for the local NBI officers from Cagayan De Oro who were waiting at court, there was a whole bunch of people from the National Television of the Philippines and other Medias, in addition to my friends and of course my attorney. I was interviewed shortly, and then suddenly the unexpected happened, the clerk handed me a clearance from all charges without even a court hearing. So, the prosecutor seemed not to be able to implement the maximum penalty as she threatened, and it was so obvious that the NBI officers were extremely pissed and were wondering how come? The plot was baked so perfectly, so how come it got burned? The look of disappointment on their faces could be read from miles away.

After I left the court with the clearance in my hand, I went straight to book a plane ticket to Manila, because I just couldn't stay in Cagayan De Oro City any longer, most especially because I didn't feel safe at all. The same day I flew to Manila, and at the airport, I went to claim the luggage that was kept there after the terrible incident of forcefully taking my kids away. My ex-wife and her family members played it right and simply knew how things are done there, having the right connections and the right amount of money was all they needed to move things around and screw me up.

I really felt so defeated, yet I refused to give up, so I went to a government official who is supposed to be responsible for severe cases like mine. So, I explained to him how people in power bent and manipulated the law, and my kids were the victims going through all this trauma, I spoke with him while my voice was shaky, and my eyes were filled with tears. In the end, he said the following: "If you were holding another passport, other than the Jordanian or any other from the third world countries, your case would have gone a totally different direction."

As much as his words were hurtful, but probably he was somewhat right, yet it was strange coming from an official of a third-world country as well.

He gave me the option to file a complaint against the officers who escorted me from Manila to Cagayan De Oro city, however, he didn't really encourage me, on the contrary, he mentioned that it could lead to consequences such as safety matters. So, the bottom line was to simply let go, because no one will help. Just imagine how this feels, you want to fight, but you are an army of one, and not only that, you have to fight on multiple fronts with limited resources and almost no connections. I left the building not knowing what should be my next move, what else could I possibly do? Thoughts were crossing my mind while walking on the sidewalks, I felt like one of the walking dead, I had no destination at all, not for the moment and neither for the near or far future. In fact the word future seemed so far-fetched, I didn't even believe that this word "future" actually exists in my dictionary after all these nerve-racking and exhausting events. Suddenly, my phone rang, a private number appeared on my Nokia screen, and when I answered, the speaker said: "all it takes is a bullet coming from a thug who's trying to get some money from a foreigner" and he immediately hang up.

Well, I wasn't surprised to be threatened, they knew that I am a very determined person and it bothered them a lot. But to be life threatened, was a hard pill to swallow.

I can't deny the fact that I was somewhat scared, but I tried to calm myself down by analyzing the situation, if they really wanted to eliminate me, they didn't need to threaten me, they would've just found ways to do so. This thought helped somehow, however, I was on a constant watch out for my surrounding, as the saying goes "better to be safe than sorry".

On the way back to my hotel, I passed by a casino just to use the toilet, and on the floor, someone must have dropped a chip that was worth 1000 Pesos, an equivalence of 20 US Dollars. I took the chip and went to the Roulette tables, I just wanted to get rid of the chip, since I wasn't intending to play in the first place. I looked at the wheel and all the numbers were either black or red, except for the number zero which was green, So, I said to myself, "I reached zero in my current life, yet it's the only number that is green, a color that represents harmony, tranquility, and peace, so it's a color of hope" And with this thought, I placed the chip on zero and turned my back. Seconds later the dealer said "Zero". What can I say other than "WoW" I just made 35,000 Pesos, equivalent to 700 US $ from a chip that I found in the bathroom!

I cashed it out and left the place immediately, then I went to my hotel and paid for my room in advance. Meanwhile, I was thinking about everything that was happening to me. I don't know if I came to the right conclusion, but I thought that no matter how many doors close in your face, there is always a door open for you, your legs might take you to a place without even planning it, and there you get what awaits you. I needed the money badly, and there it was, something to keep me rolling for a few more days in Manila until I decide what to do next, most especially after the threat that I received.

At night I couldn't sleep, not even a bit, my mind, soul, and heart kept visualizing my kids, yet I was powerless and clueless, I just didn't know what else I possibly could do. The next morning I called up the Jordanian consulate and asked them if I could leave some of my bags there since I wouldn't be able to take all of the luggage with me to Jordan, three bags belong to my kids who were supposed to be with me, but sadly that wasn't the case anymore.

Later that day I went to the consulate and left my kids' bags there, it simply didn't make any sense to take the belongings of my kids when they themselves are not with me. I spoke with the consul and tried to find means to continue the legal battle, so he suggested to consult with an attorney in Manila about the chances to file a case to the Supreme court in the Philippines, and therefore he requested from me a detailed email which I sent to him on February 20, 2013. I waited and waited for any positive results, but this attempt never saw the daylight. So, when I realized that my stay in Manila is not helping me at all, besides the feeling of being hunted made me decide to return.

A few days later in March 2013, I flew to Jordan, not because I wanted to, I just had no alternatives at that point.

Of course, my family was very happy to have me, and I was also happy to see them and be with them, despite the fact that I knew deep inside me that this is not where I wanted to be, life in Jordan is simply tough and I always had these flashbacks from the second half of my childhood; But what can you do when you have no alternatives? I was simply broke, mentally and financially, coping and surviving was the name of the game, I was trying hard not to get into depression because I knew if that happens it will be the beginning of my end.

So, I started finding means to continue the legal battle, but this time from Jordan which is a safer place compared to the Philippines where I was life threatened.

On December 08, 2013, I contacted the Department of State, The Children's Abduction Unit, and my email to them was the following:

"Dear Sir, Madam,

My name is Ahmed Khalaf and just recently last March I returned to Amman-Jordan from the Philippines. The American Embassy in Amman advised me to contact you regarding my case.

I have 3 children namely Aladdin Khalaf, Amir Khalaf, and Aziz Khalaf. Aziz is my youngest son and is an American Citizen.

I have filed a kidnapping case against my ex-wife in the Philippines in May 2012 and after thorough investigation the city prosecutor found probable cause for the kidnapping and issued a resolution to that regard in November 2012. However, due to the extreme corruption and extreme influence of my ex-in laws, once the resolution landed in court the Judge dismissed it without even a single hearing. (The Uncle of my ex-wife is a Retired Judge)

Once I couldn't fight any more in courts since everything was obviously sold out, I had to leave the Philippines for the sake of SAFETY, I was threatened and had no choice but to leave.

When I left, she was obviously more free to make whatever documents she needed to perfect her crime and legalize it.

I heard recently that she was able to get them out of the Philippines to the United States, so I wanted to make sure whether it is true or not?

The American Embassy in Manila is fully aware of my case from A to Z; However, as to what I have understood is that their hands are tight due to the lack of jurisdiction on one hand, and with whatever documents she was able to obtain UNDER THE TABLE after I left the Philippines and submitted to the Embassy, has to be honored on the other hand.

Now if she is really in the USA, I will be able to fight it through LEGIT COURTS where she will NOT be able to BRIBE anymore and has no influence either.

So Please HELP me with this complicated issue. I haven't seen my kids nor heard anything about them since February 2013.

I can provide you with all information that you may need regarding my ex-wife and my abducted children.

Looking forward hearing from you the soonest possible.

Thank you so much in advance and GOD BLESS."

I received a very quick response, right the next day on December 09, 2013, however, the response did not help me at all, the following was the reply:

"Dear Mr. Ahmed Khalaf,

Thank you for contacting the Department of State, Office of Children's Issues.

By way of background, the United States is a partner to an international treaty called the Hague Convention on International Child Abduction. Unfortunately, the

Philippines is not a treaty partner and the remedies available under the treaty will not be available to you. We will do our best to provide general information to you on the subject of international parental child abduction, but please understand there are fewer tools and resources available to you without the Hague Convention as a remedy.

We encourage you to visit our website, www.travel.state. gov, at any time to receive more information regarding the issue of international parental child abduction. I've listed the resources available to you in the United States below. Please let me know if you have any questions or concerns after reviewing the information below."

Of course I read all the options that were included in that email, however, I found myself at a dead end road, so, I decided to call them up and speak to the person rather than emailing, and I was told that my best bet would be to hire a damn good lawyer in the USA if I wanted to have some real results.

Of course, I want some real, positive results, and for that reason, I started to search right and left for attorneys and email them, but of course, how can anything in my life just go easy? I received some responses that sounded very promising, however, the least offer I got was 10,000 USD as a retainers fee at a rate of 400 USD/hour. With these figures in front of my eyes, I knew that my efforts are being wasted just like a person who's trying to grind water, when you have no resources and no one to help you, when you feel that you are even running out of ideas, you will feel that the world is just against you and for reasons you have no clue about. I honestly didn't know what to do anymore, yet something deep inside of me refused to give up, refused to surrender, refused to lose hope.

From that point on I decided to stand strong and build myself from scratch, if I was to keep whining about my past and all that had happened to me, nothing at all would ever change, that's a fact that I had and have to live with. So, my first step was to contact a Saudi man whom I met in my last days in Manila, I actually had a job interview with him, he was at that time in Manila to recruit teachers from the Philippines for his English Language Institutes, and he was also looking for a branch manager. During my meeting with this man, I understood that he was facing many problems with his Filipino teachers and that he didn't know what to do. So, we agreed to be in touch once I am back in Jordan, and that's what I did.

Meanwhile, my family got a visit from some relatives who reside in Israel, among them is a young lady who is a distant cousin of mine. One evening we went out to a shopping mall where I started talking about the past events that I have been through in the Philippines, she was very attentive and also very interested to hear what I had to say. Surprisingly, the evening went very well, despite that I always kept myself distant as much as I could from my relatives, whether they were close or distant.

Then I told her about my plans flying to Saudi Arabia as an attempt to stand on my feet once again. And indeed, that's what had happened.

At first, I wanted to test the waters, so I went there in June 2013 for 3 months. Right upon my arrival I met the head teacher of the Institute's main branch, and as per my agreement with the owner of the Institute, I requested not to present myself as the manager of the Institute, but rather as an inspector whose duty is to inspect the quality of education at all the centers of that area. In other words, I am not employed by this man but rather employed by the State. The reason why I did this was an attempt to figure out some of the problems this owner is facing, I needed to gather information as an outsider who is not related in any way to the company.

And indeed, within the first 45 minutes, I was able to identify parts of the plot that was going on at the owner's institutes. Apparently, the head teacher was extremely trusted by the owner and his partner, which he used to his advantage. When I presented myself as an inspector, this head teacher started to talk really badly about the owners and about the institutes, he further added that the teachers are exhausted and overworked. I was just listening and taking notes, and from time to time I asked a few questions to encourage him to talk further. He was trying so hard to give the worst image possible about the situation in general. From here I knew that something rotten was going on, most especially that this head teacher has been working for the institutes for 5 years, if his words were true, then why would he stay with them for so long? and so I requested to speak with all the other teachers but individually.

In the end I found out that the head teacher was the head of the snake, who had a few other teachers assisting him in implementing the plot.

It was a sort of a Mafia in an academic establishment, every new teacher who comes from the Philippines either joins their group or becomes an outcast, which turns his life into a living hell. They didn't want to have more than 10 students in a classroom, wherein the maximum number does not exceed under any circumstance 20 students. They had a set of rules that all teachers needed to stick to if they didn't want to be become an outcast, these rules were set in order to prevent the institutes from further developing, since that would only mean that there will be more workload on them, that is how the head teacher and his accomplices manipulated the minds of the new and existing teachers.

Once I had the complete picture, I presented my findings to the owner and his partner, at first, they thought that I am crazy and that I must have interpreted the whole thing wrongly. But when I told them the details and how the head teacher tried to drag their reputation through the mud, and how I was able to retrieve different information from all the teachers I spoke to, they looked at each other and said "We have Satan in the house and believed we had an Angel?!, we've been struggling for a couple of years and you found out the problem on your first day? How the heck did you do that?"

I smiled and I humbly said, "I lived in the Philippines for more than 9 years, I finished my education there, and I've been through so called shit machine, I learned their culture in and out and can tell when someone is trying to pull my leg."

In the Filipino culture there is this crab mentality which I mentioned before, when they know someone who is really good at something or succeeded in something, regardless if the person is a relative, a friend or even just an acquaintance, they will do their best to drag him or her down, they will make their lives so miserable just to succeed in destroying what the person has achieved or stop the person from progressing. And so was the case with all these new teachers who came to Saudi Arabia motivated and willing to work, just to end up being manipulated. Of course, if the talent of some teacher will be discovered, that will show and reflect the weaknesses of the others, in particular the gang leaders, for that reason they decided to come up with this dirty plan to let the institutes run, but only to a certain limit, they were in a complete control.

When I was asked by the management how I learned about the crab mentality, I told them that I learned it the hard way, it cost me losing my kids, since my ex-wife was partly a victim by this terrible practice among most Filipinos, where her so called family, friends and even acquaintances were so extremely jealous of her, they constantly poured poison in her ears. Of course this is not an excuse for what she has done, yet it's undeniably an additional reason to her satanic actions.

There was a whole lot of tension at the institutes' main branch when they discovered that I am the new education manager, the news quickly spread to all the other branches and the tension just grew hour by hour. No one knew what will happen next, except me, I intended to clean up the filth in the company. So, I visited all the branches and gathered further information and spoke to all the teachers and head teachers, just to find out that the majority were under the umbrella of the main branch's head teacher.

The process of gathering information, analyzing, and discussing the findings with the owners took about a week, and then I decided to cut the head of the snake as a first move to clean up the filth. The head teacher got fired and was sent back home to the Philippines, yet he received all his rights as if he had done nothing bad, that was the generosity of the owners who despite the harm caused by him, and his accomplices was treated as if nothing happened. This move was a shock to all, no one ever expected for this to happen to their leader, yet it was a relief to many as well who were forced to be part of the group.

Right the next day after the departure of the head teacher, the owners came to the main branch and noticed the change in the air, it was not electrified anymore, it was truly a different environment, so peaceful and tranquil.

The owners smiled and said, "we are speechless, you proved us wrong Ahmed, you found the problem and solved it in a timely manner, we sense and see the difference, what would we do without you?"

Honestly, these words meant a lot to me, having the feeling of being appreciated, the acknowledgment of the work that has been done, the results that were achieved in a very short time, all of this was an assurance for me that I should keep doing what I was doing and to the best of my ability. I needed to stay focused, I needed to remind myself that only me can help myself at this point of time, life has been a roller coaster for me, but that is not a reason to give up, life goes on, it's never the end until it's the end.

Working at the institutes was very challenging yet fulfilling, my only problem was the environment of the region, extremely hot and humid, on the streets you mainly see men, and if you see any women, they are always covered up in black from head to toe, it was depressing and didn't feel natural at all, but what can you do? This is the culture of the land, either you go along with it and try to adjust yourself, or you say Hasta La vista baby. The truth to be said, the only time I longed for Jordan was during the time I was in the Eastern part of Saudi Arabia. It's kind of ironic, since Jordan was never a place I wanted to be at, except for the time that I spent working at the language centers in Saudi Arabia.

My three trial months seemed like three centuries, not because of work, but because of the lifestyle that I am not and never will be used to. The accomplishments however were tremendous, I established an HR department and set rules for all the employees including the owners. I fired a total of 5 teachers and hired 6 during this period.

What somehow eased my stay in Saudi Arabia was my constant communication with my distant cousin, she was so supportive ever since we had that evening out together. She just came into my life at the right moment, I needed someone like her, someone I can talk to openly without being judged, someone who understands what it means to be at rock bottom and trying to get up by any means possible. She Just understood me more than anyone else I have ever met in my entire life. What a timing, huh? It surprises me, how this world actually functions, there are times when you think it's the end , but it's just a delusion that you get trapped in due to the severe circumstances that you are going through, but if just give yourself the chance to believe that everything happens for a reason, whether you find it out or not is not the point, it's just the belief itself, because that is what will make you see and find a new path that you have not expected nor planned. Indeed there is always a door open.

And then, finally the day has come to leave. The owner who I met in Manila was the one to personally drive me to the airport, he said many nice words to me and also gave me extra money above my salary. I was really touched, most especially when he said, "Ahmed, you were never an employee in my eyes, nor in my partner's eyes, you are and always will be a friend and a brother, we wholeheartedly appreciate what you have done for us, and I hope that you will think about working with me and my partner, we need you"

I thanked him for his nice words and appreciation, we shook hands and parted ways.

Days after my arrival to Jordan in September 2013, I applied to take a course called ICDL which stands for International Computer Driver's License, I just wanted to fill my time with something productive, and at the same time gain as much experience as possible in various fields. Meanwhile, I kept working for my Saudi friend from a distance, but it wasn't really a job, I just helped them from time to time whenever they needed something.

By January 2014, I finished my course and took the corresponding exam which I passed pretty easily, which is actually strange, since almost nothing in my life was ever easy, was it a shift? Was it a new era? I really have no idea, but it made me happy to have some positive moments in my life, that only meant that I was hopefully on the right path.

In February my relatives came to visit us again, and it seemed that there was a spark between me and my distant cousin, and indeed it was. Despite that my heart was not ready to start a new relationship since I was still traumatized and not believing that I would ever be with someone again. I had this feeling that I just have no luck with women. But I decided not to limit myself and not to let the past affect my future, what happened just happened, there is nothing in my power to change the past, I can only learn from it and work on being the best that I can be.

So, without wasting any time, I just broke all the natural rules of opening a sensitive topic to another person, I just bluntly told her, "listen, I am hurt, and I have no idea what to do next, I have no idea if I can trust anyone ever again, I have feelings for you, but I honestly don't know if that is love or not, maybe it's just a feeling of appreciation that you stood by my side without having any expectations, or maybe I just developed that feeling because you listened to me without throwing any judgments, I have no clue"

She smiled at me and said, "Are you proposing to me? Is that a new style or what?"

I didn't think twice, and I answered with a yes, it was indeed a proposal, maybe weird, but from experience, even when you plan something and you think that you have covered everything, there is no assurance that things will work exactly as planned, there is always that element of surprise, simply because you don't know people unless you had the chance to find out their reactions in different life settings, different locations and most importantly outside of their comfort zone. Only then you might say that you know the person, yet there is still no guarantee that you know him or her inside out. Life just doesn't work that way.

I can say that a new chapter in my life started from that point on, she said "yes" and so we got engaged on February 25, 2014. The process of engagement wasn't easy at all though, since my fiancé is an Israeli citizen and the engagement found place in Jordan, I had to get a permit from the ministry of interior first. As much as it might sound strange, in the end, it is what is, these are the rules of the country, and we simply have to follow them.

A few days later, she went back home with her family and I started looking for a job, which I surprisingly found pretty fast, but all it took was one month for me to be out again, the owners of the language center gave me less money than what was agreed upon, so, with that, I came to a final conclusion, I will never ever try again seeking belongingness to a place that I don't belong to, or don't feel as part of it. The only reason I was there was because I had no alternatives in different periods of my life, despite that my family is settled there, whether they like it or not, they don't talk about it, they just go with the flow I guess, but that was not the case with me. What really pissed me off all my life is how my lovely parents made mistakes that not only affected their lives but mainly affected the lives of their children. It all started with my grandparents who lived all their lives in Israel, my grandmother from my mom's side once exchanged 21,000 square feet of land for a Holland cow which died in less than a year after obtaining it. Seriously, isn't that so stupid?! It's true that I am talking about my grandmother here, and it sounds very rude to say this, but the fact doesn't really change, does it? Who in his right mind exchanges land that is worth millions of dollars for a living creature? My mom could have had a very decent living from the land they owned which was so easily thrown away. And it's not a different case with my grandfather from my dad's side, who also had no less than 80,000 square feet of land which apparently wasn't registered with the Israeli authorities after the establishment of the State of Israel.

And not only that, my mom in her teenage years, when she was engaged to my dad who already flew to Germany ahead of her, followed an extremely stupid piece of advice from her parents to give up her Israeli citizenship in order to follow my dad to Germany through Jordan rather than from Tel Aviv. I just don't understand what they were thinking.

And when my parents got together and established their family, they never obtained their German citizenship despite that they lived over 25 years there, and that's another huge mistake they committed, which not only affected them, but it affected us as children. One day my mom decided that she wants to leave Germany, and since she couldn't return to her original place which is Israel due to the stupid and insane advice of surrendering her Israeli citizenship which she naively followed, we ended up being taken to a place that we have no ties to. It seems that it didn't affect my sisters that much since they were 5 and 6 years younger than me, but for me, it really hit me hard. I was never able to accept, and I was never able to forgive my parents for that move. If you really want to move to another country, then at least take us to where we truly belong, or take us to a place where maybe we could have some chances of getting a decent life. But how could they? they couldn't.

Jordan could be a fantastic place for many people, especially for the rich ones, and it could be a great place for those who were born there and know nothing else, which made them get used to living there. It is also an amazing tourist destination, however, for me, it was just the place where I got traumatized as a child, and it stayed with me my entire life. For that reason, I only stayed in Jordan whenever I couldn't escape, and I used every opportunity to make that escape happen.

So, my next escape was when I got a job offer in July 2014 as a professional English teacher in an English academy in Istanbul-Turkey. A representative of the academy waited for me at the airport, it seemed to be a good start, but when I reached the shared apartment for teachers, I met 2 of them who were packing their stuff, so I introduced myself and they did the same. Then I asked them about the academy, and they answered that the students were good. This answer didn't seem right, there was something hidden and I had to find it out myself.

Life in Turkey was really cool, I genuinely enjoyed it, and the students were also amazing, so, the teachers were right, but, and here it comes, the owner of the academy was a real crook. They had this system that they will keep the teachers' first month's salary so that if someone decides to leave them after discovering their bad management, and their twisted methods, they will be forced to stay because the academy has a whole month's salary in their pockets, which will not be given until the lapse of the contract period which is one year. This means, whoever works for them has to have enough money to survive for 2 months from his/her own pocket until the first salary will be received in the second month. Whoever doesn't have money to survive until the second month, has to borrow from them an amount that cannot exceed 50% of the salary that is being held. And if someone thinks that he/she is tough enough and wants to leave sooner, then fine, by all means, however, all the expenses they shouldered in coming to Turkey, as well as the expenses during the first month from eating to drinking and transportation, and on top of that a whole month of working will be gone in thin air. So basically that meant that I was stuck working at a company where only the students were nice, everything else was truly terrible.

I was so furious and utterly pissed off, why are these things happening to me? Why can't I just land a decent job where no twisted methods are being used? So, I reminded myself that nothing should stop me from becoming the best I can be, regardless of the obstacles on my way, and regardless of the villains I meet during my life journey, eventually, things have to become better. With that thought I decided to leave during the third month, so, in the first month I borrowed 50% of my salary that was held, and in the second month I borrowed the other half, and in the third, I only worked for a few days which I didn't get paid for, so I considered it as a charity for the poor academy that is trying so hard to make some extra bucks from the teachers who entrusted them. So disgusting how some companies run their businesses.

Nevertheless, the time spent in Istanbul-Turkey was just fantastic, however, the time had come, and in October 2014 I booked a flight to Jordan, and once again back to where I didn't want to be.

Well, now I was in Jordan, jobless, engaged but not with my fiancé, still responsible for the child support of my first disastrous marriage, and the cherry on the top of the pie, my heart that was torn because I had no clue about my kidnapped children, almost 2 years passed without any news about them, not even the slightest bit.

If it wasn't for my father's support, I would've been totally screwed, he was actually the one who helped me from to time to cover the required children's support. It's actually so ironic, having 3 children who live close by, yet they seem so far away. I honestly don't blame them since they only know what their mom told them, but I was hopeful that the days to come will clear my name. And the irony continues, to have another batch of 3 kids who have been forcefully taken away, yet nothing could be done, nor do I know anything about them. Sometimes I wonder, how much can a human being handle? For God's sake, I am not Superman, the load is way too heavy, what else am I supposed to do? How can I cope with all of this? Questions after question were blitzing in my head.

Thankfully I was in constant communication with my fiancé who truly supported me all the way, yet, her hands were tight, she also was waiting to get the approval from the Ministry of Interior in Israel to issue me a fiancé visa. The process was very hard, slow, and even complicated, so, there was nothing that we could do besides wait.

But do you know how hard it is just to wait when you don't have a specific time frame? It's like being tortured on a daily basis without ever knowing if there will be a stop to it or not.

Suddenly the strangest thing happened, my step mom dreamed that there was gold hidden in the backyard of our house, this is still not strange on the contrary, it's just a dream, but what makes it strange is that my dad, one of my sisters, and a friend of ours who lived nearby, all had the same dream at the same night.

I was like a drowning person who holds unto a straw, I wanted to take action immediately, it was like an adrenalin pump, here it is, here is the time to finally breathe, my hopes were high, and I just wanted to start digging, but in a backyard that is almost 5000 square feet big, the question was, where to start? I took these dreams really seriously, I wanted to believe in them, so I hired someone who has a metal detector device to show me where to start, but I have to admit that I committed a big mistake because you can't just trust people that easily, the guy started drooling and said "if you manage to get it out, don't forget to give me some" his words were confusing, I didn't really understand what exactly he meant, why did he say "if you manage to get it out"?

On the same day I started digging and for a few days everything was still normal, but once I reached approximately 3 feet, my used digging tools didn't help anymore, so I needed a Hydraulic Drilling compressor machine, which I was able to rent. It surely helped a lot to accomplish more, in fact in about one month I reached 15 feet deep, but the downside of it was that it made people around me, the so called nosy neighbors threaten to call the authorities if they didn't get a cut. I just find this so disgusting; no one leaves you alone, everybody around you wants something from you, everybody is eying on you and on your movements. You are not allowed to become better than them, if they are down you have to stay at rock bottom just like them. I didn't even know that digging in your own property is forbidden in Jordan! Wow? I was so frustrated, so angry, so pissed off, I could smell wealth, but your disgusting neighbors and the authorities will not allow you to reach your aim. Now I understood what the guy meant with his statement. "if you manage to get it out".

I knew that even if I would find the treasure, it might be just a curse, because there were too many eyes monitoring every single move I made. Besides, I didn't want to do anything that is illegal, my life is already messed up without breaking any laws, so how would it be if I did break some laws? It's just not worth it, at least not to me. So, I decided to stop, and all my hard work evaporated.

Days and months have passed, until July 2015, and to be exact, it was July 15 when I received an expected email. Not even in my wildest dreams would I have expected this turn of events. At least it gave me some sort of hope, something that I could hold unto.

Dear Mr. Ahmed Khalaf,

I am of People's Television Network, Manila, Philippines (PTV4). I got your contact details from the Consul of the Jordanian Consulate.

At this moment, the Philippines is taking into consideration in to the Accession on the Hague Convention on International Child Abduction. Last week, Ambassador Susan Jacobs had visited the Philippines for a Forum and discussed to the concerned government authorities about the Hague Abduction Convention.

During the forum here in the Philippines, your case was presented as an example of this International Child Abduction.

Currently, our Documentary Program, The Veronica Chronicles is doing a comprehensive discussion regarding the International Child Abduction.

With this, we would like to have a Skype Interview with you to tell us more of your story. Rest assured that your identity will be treated with confidentiality.

The skype interview will be on July 16, 2015, at 10AM (Jordan Time).

Hope to have you in this episode.

You can reach me through the contact details below my signature.

Thank you.

After reading this email, I had mixed feelings, a combination of pain and relief simultaneously, so, I replied to their email with my acceptance. The next day the interview was held, and I got the chance to share bits of my painful story.

The interview was aired on public television in the Philippines, and since that time it was posted online under PINOY CROSS-BORDER KIDS [July 2015 Episode]. The language used is a mix of Tagalog and English.

After the online video became available, I started writing all the departments that I contacted in 2013 once again, but this time with a copy of the video link. Yet, it shouldn't be a surprise anymore, nothing at all helped, there was no progress whatsoever. On the contrary, it just added to my pain, because my spirit that was lifted up for a while was smashed into the core of earth.

Just a couple of days later I received a phone call from my Saudi Boss, and without any introductions he said, "Ahmed, we need you, honestly you have no excuses, you must come" considering my current situation, I was not in a state to play hard to get, and so I told him to send me the visa. It took about 45 days to complete the needed documents, since this time I was not going to Saudi Arabia on a temporary visa, but rather as a resident. By September 2015 I started working with the Institutes again, but this time it was kind of easier than the first time, most especially that I already knew what was waiting for me and what to expect.

I spent most of my time working, just to avoid thinking about the past events, I just wanted to focus on making some money and paying back my dad, even if it was just a part of what I owed him.

My responsibilities at the Institutes were endless, but I worked with them as if it was my own place, they made me feel like part of the family, and I was well compensated for the efforts that I exerted. It would be even a shame to compare them with my last 2 workplaces in Jordan and Turkey because there is simply no comparison.

During my stay I worked as an HR manager, an Education Consultant, and a teacher's trainer, I was even responsible for implementing all the changes that were happening on a constant basis.

In December 2015, I flew with my boss to Malta to meet with some managers of a well-known language school. The idea was to send the Institutes' students there during summertime for a period of 4 weeks. So, we had to check the places and discuss the program and events that were offered. It was a very successful trip, wherein we got to know and meet many interesting people. I have to say that I was quite surprised that the trip went smoothly with no obstacles since I am very much used to having some spicy events no matter where I go to. I don't know if life wanted to give me some sort of a break, or was it just pure luck?

Whatever it was, I am thankful that I had a really good time with my boss who from that point on became my closest friend. It's not that common to become friends with your boss, and I mean really close friends, but what is common in my life anyway?

With hard work and perseverance, there was a noticeable income increase for the institutes of about 25%, which made the owners very happy. In April 2015 I went with my boss to Ukraine in order to recruit English teachers in an attempt of finding substitutes for the teachers from the Philippines. It was not an easy task at all, hence most people we got to interview had a strong accent, and those who had almost no accent were not convinced to leave Ukraine and settle in Saudi Arabia for a couple of years, I truly don't blame them at all. Yet, there was one unique teacher who had the whole package, accent free, very kind, polite, and extremely helpful. He even escorted us to visit some other cities besides Kyiv. Sadly that such kinds of people are very rare these days, but it was probably our luck, or rather my luck to at least have achieved something during this trip. So, we signed the contract with this teacher and gave him the list of requirements that he needs to work on, in order for him to obtain a visa to Saudi Arabia.

Two days before our flight back to Saudi Arabia, my boss went out by himself, and suddenly my phone rang, it was him, he gave me his location and told me to come quickly. I took a cap and went to the address that he provided me with, I was kind of nervous, most especially because he told me to be quick. Once I arrived, I saw him seated with 2 guys who were from the middle east. The guys were trying to convince my boss to do business with them, and for that reason, he called me to take my opinion. As we were talking I noticed one of the guys winking to the other, then the other guy asked my boss to go with him to a shop nearby to show him something, meanwhile, the second guy told me "listen, your boss is Saudi, he has money and he is convinced doing business with us, so don't be a deal breaker, I promise you that we will give you a fair cut from what we will earn"

I smiled at him and told him "this person whom you are talking about is not only my boss, but he is my closest friend, so watch your mouth and weigh your words, money comes and goes, but a good person once gone, you might never find him or her again" The guy started laughing and said, "You are so dramatic, life is all about money my friend" So I answered him "Firstly I am not your friend, and secondly, you are entitled to your opinion which you cannot impose on me, and lastly he is a grown-up man who can decide for himself".

I was really pissed off, but I didn't want to show my anger, especially since I had no clue who these guys were and what they were capable of. When my boss came back with the other guy, he was actually in a good mood and wanted me to give my opinion right away, despite that I had no clue what the heck the business was all about. So, I told him that I would not be able to do so unless I know what the proposal is all about, apparently, they had two proposals, the first one was exporting sunflower oil to Saudi Arabia, which still sounded all right, but the second one was the straw that broke the camel's back, they were talking about using people in need who would be ready to sell one of their kidneys for people who need a transplant. To make it sound fantastic and acceptable, they mentioned that it's all done in a known hospital and that they will provide translation for those who don't speak Russian or English, in addition, they offered help in getting accommodation. As sweet as the offered services sounded, I knew that there was something behind it, they committed two mistakes that made me alert, the first one was when the guys winked at each other, and the second one was when the guy spoke to me and tried to bribe me with a fair cut; if they were legit, they didn't need to beat around the bush like that.

I had to think fast to escape the scene, but at the same time, I didn't want the guys to notice that I am pulling the rag from underneath their feet. So, I called myself from one phone to the other, and when I answered the mysterious call, I said, "Yes, yes, we will be there on time, it will just take us about 20 minutes". My boss was looking at me wondering, and before he was able to open his mouth, I told him that we have to be at the recruiting agency for our appointment. I was able to sense at that moment that he was about to say that we had no meeting and that we were free. So, before giving him the chance to do so, I told him that we have a new batch of teachers who are waiting for us to be interviewed. This is my boss's kryptonite, he just loves to interview teachers in the hope to find as many qualified teachers as possible, but at the same time with a reasonable cost as to his say.

In order to let everything appear normal, I requested to have the phone number of the guy who spoke to me, and I gave him my temporary Ukrainian phone number. We shook hands and finally parted ways.

As soon as we were inside a cap, I exploded in the face of my boss, he was so shocked and extremely surprised, but when I told him about everything he said: "Oh my brother, what will I do without you? no words can describe my appreciation". Nice words and soothing, but I just didn't want to be in such a situation ever again, because there is never an assurance that it will end well when you meet up with people who make a living from Scams and other illegal ways and methods.

Despite that, we met those crooks in Ukraine on the last two days of our stay, but it was still a beautiful and successful trip, and quite honestly, I didn't want to return to Saudi Arabia, but that was just my dream. A couple of weeks after our return, two events happened, the first one was not good news from the Ukrainian teacher whom we signed a contract with, the poor guy discovered during the required medical examination for obtaining a working visa for Saudi Arabia that he had HIV, which hindered him from getting the approval. The second event was good news for me, but it wasn't good for my bosses, I finally got the fiancé visa approval from Israel which I could obtain from The Israeli embassy in Jordan, which meant that I will be leaving Saudi Arabia for good. It was such a happy moment for me, since it was the first step of a long unknown path that may lead to obtaining my original right of being in the land where my family belonged to.

As a farewell gift, I received an extra month salary from my friend-boss, and I also got an iPad from his partner. They also had a farewell party to which everyone was invited, and I received an amazingly beautiful, framed certificate. Now this is a place that appreciates hard and smart work, it's a place that you will always remember. My only negative comment about it would be the location, but that is something that can't be changed, since that is the place, they originated from.

In late May 2016, I was already in Jordan, my fiancé and her family came in the first week of June, and then finally the day has come, on June 15, 2016, I entered the homeland of my parents and grandparents, the homeland of my fiancé and her parents. It doesn't matter what words I use here to describe the feeling, there is no language on planet earth that has the needed vocabulary to reflect or to explain the feelings I had on that day.

With this turn of events, I was asking myself many questions, "Is this the path that will change my life? Is this the path that will make me happy despite my endless sorrows? Is this the path that will give me the chance to be reunited with my kidnapped kids? Is this the path that will restore my faith in relationships?"

I guess only time could answer these questions, so I decided to wait and see what the future had hidden for me. On July 13, 2016, we had a wedding, and we were officially announced as husband and wife.

If you expect to read what happened that night, that's not going to happen, just use your imagination.

Just a couple of month later, my wife discovered that she got pregnant, which was actually not planned at all, we were not ready for this, we were just starting from scratch, but it's actually no brainer anymore, things happen regardless of being planned or not.

The start was extremely hard in Israel, for one, I wasn't allowed to work yet, so I was jobless and was almost fully dependent on my wife and her family, which is definitely not a wonderful feeling. Secondly, the city I lived in is a very tough place, and thirdly and most importantly I had endless interviews at the ministry of interior in order to get my residency and to be allowed to work. Every time we had to provide new documents and, on the day, when we had a meeting, we had to wait for hours and hours.

If it wasn't for my wife's support, I might have given up, because everything was just pressuring me, everything had to be so hard, yet no one could explain why? I wanted to do so many things with my life, but the obstacles kept coming and it seemed that there is never an end to them.

I spent almost my first year like that, trying with my wife to get at least a work permit. And finally, in 2017 I got my temporary residency which entitled me to work freely. At last, I got some freedom, but I still had some restrictions, such as my inability to work at the Jewish sector due to my limited knowledge of Hebrew, furthermore, we only had one car which was used by my wife, so going to work via public transportation could consume a whole lot of time due to traffic jam issues.

So, my only option was to work in the city we lived in, and from here I slowly started to discover what kind of a rotten society the city has, of course that does not mean all of the people, yet a huge number of them. At first, it didn't bother me much, because things were still bearable, or maybe because I didn't discover everything yet.

On April 25, 2017, my daughter was born and with that, a new member entered the family. With my daughter's birth, I learned a new lesson, it doesn't matter how much you worry, it doesn't matter if you are ready or not; when something is meant to happen then it will happen, the lesson is, you'll never know if it's the right time or not until you live it out. See, life is full of mysteries, some we understand and figure out, and some we never do. A couple of months after my daughter's birth a few things happened that I never expected, nor did plan for. My daughter in Jordan who is my eldest child and was all the while so distant from me, called me up and said "Dad, now I have a sister, and it makes me happy, but I will always be your first daughter" She really made me cry, despite that her words were simple and normal, but as a father who didn't have the chance to be around his kids for so many different reasons, the words had such a great impact on me. Firstly, with her nice voice calling me Dad, and secondly acknowledging her sister, and last but not least, showing some innocent jealousy that she's no longer the only girl. My daughter's birth opened a path to be connected with my lovely kids in Jordan after such a long time. My thoughts started wandering, would it be possible that one day I will be united with all my kids? Will I ever find my kids who have no presence online, it's been almost 5 years now that I know nothing about them.

The second thing that happened which was so unplanned, I applied and got accepted to take up my master's degree at Tel Aviv University. Without even thinking of any consequences, my lovely wife took a loan from the bank so that I could pay the fees. She is just like me, she adores education and that's why she didn't hesitate to take this move. This is simply how life is, some people are more privileged than others, I always wanted to pursue my studying, but my chances were very limited, and the obstacles just made it impossible. For other people, it might be much easier due to various reasons, but I just wasn't one of those other people.

Yet, because I didn't give up and I kept following my aim and my dream, it eventually happened without even planning it. It was just a matter of time I believe.

Before the master's program started, I had to take up a compulsory ULPAN course, which is a Hebrew language course, there I had the privilege to meet some fantastic people, and one of those people I become close friends with; she is from Switzerland and works for a well-known health organization. This friendship evolved quickly and she became a friend of my wife as well.

During the master's program, I really had fantastic instructors and really cool classmates; we got along very well. The courses were tough though because it was an intensive master's program. It seems that I stressed myself to the extreme, because one day during class I felt pain in my chest and had shortness of breath, when my wife came to pick me up in the afternoon it escalated and I felt like fainting in the car, so she took me immediately to the hospital where I got hospitalized for 2 days. The strange part is that they didn't find anything abnormal.

So, I started connecting the dots after these questions flashed in front of my eyes, how is it possible that all my life I have been struggling? Everything I do either stops or gets postponed or if I get to finish it, it's after extreme suffering, wherein when others do similar tasks, it goes smoothly. There is something that just doesn't make sense here, there is something that's missing. I started to believe that I have energy blockages, some sort of curse that needed to be cured. I tried everything, from meditation to prayers, to contacting healers, to chakra healing, you name it. The main issue was finding the right person who really has the knowledge about these things, and not a person who tells you a whole bunch of crap.

I started making my own research, because I decided to work on myself as much as I can, this chest pressure that I had was so annoying and it drained me totally out, it was not constant, but it occurred several times a day. Now just to rule out any medical condition, I made all the possible checkups, and everything turned out normal.

One thing that added to being exhausted was my newborn baby who hated sleep, she barely slept at night, and when she did, she kept waking up in between. Just imagine all of these things on your plate, you barely sleep, you have pain that you don't know where it's coming from and what causes it, this pain drains you totally out, you have to work hard for your University and add to this, being in an extremely noisy city, where people don't give a damn if you are sleeping or not, if you are sick or not, they will drift their cars or even speed with their noisy ATV vehicles in the middle of the night or even in bright daylight, seven days a week. This is something that is done by teenagers and adults. These people are simply shameless, disrespectful, no responsibility, no manners, nothing. Just disgusting.

The irony is that despite of all these negative characteristics, life was still much better from being in Jordan, at least I had open opportunities here, endless options, and chances that needed to be grabbed.

At midnight of December 13, 2017, I received the news that my dad passed away, so we immediately drove to Jordan the next morning, my old man was gone. It was so painful, this was the second time that I lost someone so close to my heart, my tears were falling, and my heart was tearing up. I stayed with him until he was buried, and after that, I couldn't speak to anyone. Surprisingly, my two sons approached me and tried to comfort me, the path has opened, a path that I didn't see coming. I think it was like a message from the Universe, it probably was telling me "Your dad is gone and there is nothing you can do about it, it's a fact that will happen to every living soul on earth. Your sons are ready to open a new page with you, they grew up and understand life much better now, take this chance, and don't waste it."

I listened to this voice, and I embraced them so tight as if there was no tomorrow. My dad passed away, but a new relationship was born with my kids in Jordan. Indeed everything happens for a reason, when my young daughter was born, my eldest daughter opened her heart, and when my dad passed away, my sons opened their hearts. I wish I had the power to understand life, there are so many twists in it, so many mysteries. Some I was able to figure out, analyze, interpret, you name it, but I still couldn't solve the riddle behind being tortured daily not knowing why my kids were kidnapped, why was I deprived from being with them, when I am the one who raised them by myself?

A few days later we went back to Israel, it wasn't easy, but life just goes on, apparently, this is how life works, today you are with your beloved ones and tomorrow you might lose them for whatever reasons.

In December I submitted my last Seminar paper at the University and with that I fulfilled all the requirements and was just waiting for my graduation which took place in March 2018. It's a beautiful feeling when you achieve something after so many hurdles and so many ups and downs.

A short while later I had to attend another appointment with my wife at the Ministry of Interior to renew my temporary residency, which meant providing the same previous documents but under a new date, as well as providing any new documents if present. I saw this as an opportunity that I have finished my master's degree, at least it will show that I am working on myself as much as I can. Thankfully the process was less complicated this time and I got the renewal pretty fast.

Two years passed already since I settled in Israel, the land of my parents and grandparents, however, I realized that being in an Arab Israeli town is totally different from being in a Jewish town, but unfortunately moving out was not an option, since it costs a fortune.

As an attempt to move forward I decided to work for myself rather than work for people who will always try to suck your blood and never show appreciation, sadly that is the case in most places where you would work. So, I created a consulting website where I offered consultation services in various domains, to be more specific, a consultation in every field in which I have been personally involved. See, when life throws you right and left, you either let it drag you down or you fight it as hard as you can and learn from it. Now, this learning becomes a solid experience.

I personally believe that the advice that you can get from someone who has gained this experience the hard way is definitely worth listening to. How I wish I knew someone who could have extended a solid piece of advice in any of my most crucial moments in life. It probably could have changed the entire course of events, who knows?

Anyway, I had to officially register the website at the ministry of commerce, and with that, I became the owner of a small startup company. Honestly, I had no expectations from this move, I just wanted anything to make me feel that I am moving forward.

A couple of months later, I had my first customer who found me through my website, he first emailed me and then asked me to contact him back if I had the time, which of course I did. When I called him, we had a little chat on the phone, he seemed very interested and requested to meet in a 5-star hotel in Tel Aviv on the same day. As much as I was thrilled, happy, and excited I was also nervous, but I didn't know why? Maybe because I never expected to have a customer? Or was it because it seemed strange to be contacted in the first place? especially since Israel has endless professional consulting companies, so why me? Well, I decided not to think about it anymore, and just go to the meeting. And I am glad that I did, he was a real gentleman, very polite, and straightforward, or maybe not that straightforward!

My task was to gather some information from the internet about some startup companies and the allotted time for this task was exactly 2 days. If you think about it a bit, it actually sounds so lame, but never judge a book by its cover, it is far from being lame and it is far from being stupid, it's just a totally different world. I know that this sounds so confusing, but I was also very confused until I learned that this was just a simple test for something much bigger to come. As much as I would love to delve deeper into this unbelievable new life experience, the associated possible risks far outweigh the benefits of mentioning any further details, and therefore, this chapter of my life closes here with the positive thought that I learned many things in person and in real life which otherwise will only come across in movies.

In September 2020, I opened my own language center for English, which was relatively easy to accomplish because this center was under the umbrella of my startup company. The only hard part was to come up with the expenses for establishing the place, but in the end, it worked.

I had several groups of students, and I can say that I had a very successful start despite of the Corona pandemic outbreak. There were even times when I had to work for seven days a week. I just wanted to utilize my time as much I could, I wanted to make as much money as possible to have the so called financial freedom, however, I know for fact that what I did was wrong, because exchanging time for money will never make anyone reach the desired financial freedom. Anyway, there were several contributing factors that made me decide taking a new path, firstly, the crime rate increased tremendously in the city I lived in, there were murders on almost a daily basis, something totally disgusting. What makes it even weirder is when the students of all ages, from grade 3 to grade 12 talk about these crimes as if it's something normal. This raised an alarm in me, and I started thinking about the alternatives, because definitely this city is not a place where I want my daughter to grow up.

Surprisingly, the doors of heaven seemed to be open and received my thoughts and converted them into possibilities. I was invited by the ministry of interior to take the oath to finally become an Israeli citizen. This event has flipped my life 180 degrees, it restored some parts of life that were broken long time ago by my grandparents and parents. This event gave me the freedom of choice and the chance to start something that I wanted to do long time ago but was never possible. Returning to the land where my lungs got their first air in, the land of my birth, the land where everything in my life has started. Indeed everything comes in due time.

So, now a new chapter of life has unfolded, I am back in Germany since 2022, and my lovely wife and daughter will follow soon.

Every beginning has something unique in it, my move to my birthland opened a path that was closed since 2014. That's the year when I started writing this book and never had the chance to finish it until something very strange happened. So strange that I became a strong believer in the nonexistence of coincidences, everything in life, good or bad happens for a reason, and you just have to fill in the blanks.

Out of the blue, I received an email from a lovely person named Hailey Clark who is a Senior Literary Manager and Marketing Consultant at Ink Start Media. Apparently, there is another person who has the exact same name as mine who wrote a book, and I was approached because she thought I was him. Now to me, this was a clear sign to step it up and finish my book, so that people can read it. There is no way in heaven that there is a coincidence that is so finely detailed, out of 8 billion people on planet earth, a guy with the same name as mine wrote a book, and I am the one to be contacted? Really? This is by no means a coincidence. But regardless of what it is, it made this book see the light.

The question now is, what will happen next? Will I ever get the chance to find my kidnapped kids who still don't have any presence on the internet? It's been almost 11 years now that I know nothing about them, is that going to change? Is there going to be a path that will lead me to them? Will my youngest daughter ever have the chance to get to know her siblings? And how about my kids in Jordan, will they get the chance to know them one day? Is it possible that life will extend its courtesy a bit further and justice will be served? How about the path that I have taken now, where will it lead me to?

There are endless questions, but I have no answers to any of them. Maybe only with time, some answers will be revealed.

Now regardless of what is going to happen in the future, a lesson is to be learned from all that I have mentioned, it's up to each and every person how to deal with life-rocking situations, but the bottom line is, try to never give up, try to stand strong for your own sake first, and never ever give your enemies the satisfaction that they were able to defeat you. They might have won a battle or even more, but that doesn't mean that you have lost the war.

You might have times when you feel that the whole world is against you, you might feel that nothing at all will ever help you, you might even feel that it's your end. But none of that really matters, just remember, there will always be a path that you can take, even if you don't know where it will lead to. You just have to try, take The Path to The Unknown and remember, NEVER GIVE UP.